Refined By The Fire(d)

"Kyle Isabelli's *Refined by the Fire(d)* is a captivating and deeply personal narrative-driven book that delves into the often unspoken reality of being fired from a church. With empathy and wisdom, Kyle shares his journey, offering solace, practical advice, and a path to healing for individuals navigating the aftermath of termination. *Refined by the Fire(d)* stands as a testament to Kyle's dedication in filling a void and providing invaluable support to those facing similar challenges."

— **Caleb Breakey,** author of *Called to Stay*

Only those who have been fired by a church can truly understand the experience of pastoral termination. Kyle Isabelli truly understands. Through his detailed account of being fired and, ultimately, being refined, Kyle takes his readers through his experience of processing the pain, finding renewed purpose, and persevering amid shock, betrayal, and intense pain. Ministers who have been fired by a church will find encouragement and healing in Kyle's story. Church leaders will find clear advice and sound strategies for firing a minister if the occasion arises. In a time when ministers are being fired at an alarming rate, *Refined by the Fire(d)* is a must read.

— **Deanna Harrison,** Executive Director,
Pastors' Hope Network

Rarely does a writer courageously open up with the level of transparency expressed in this intimate telling of Pastor Kyle's painful and unjust firing from a much-loved ministry and subsequent heart-wrenching/faith-enhancing journey toward healing. Traversing deep dives into scripture, sleepless nights wrestling with God, countless hours gleaning wisdom from trusted mentors and pastoral counselors, and the tender support and guidance from a loving spouse, Pastor Kyle assembles his journey's hard-won wisdom into this roadmap to a compassionate and practical approach for navigating difficult employment challenges. This is not just a book for the fire(d). This indispensable volume is for leaders, their direct reports, and those touched by their lives and decisions.

— **Edward P. McHugh, MSW, LCSW,**
Past President and Clinical Director of
Village Christian Counseling Center, Inc.

REFINED by the FIRE(D)

HOW TO PROCESS PAIN, REGAIN PURPOSE, & PERSEVERE AFTER BEING FIRED BY YOUR CHURCH

KYLE ISABELLI

NEW YORK

LONDON • NASHVILLE • MELBOURNE • VANCOUVER

Refined By The Fire(d)

How to Process Pain, Regain Purpose, and Persevere After Being Fired by Your Church

Published in New York, New York, by Morgan James Publishing. Morgan James is a trademark of Morgan James, LLC. www.MorganJamesPublishing.com

Proudly distributed by Publishers Group West®

ISBN 9781636981864 paperback
ISBN 9781636981871 ebook
Library of Congress Control Number: 2023935999

Cover & Interior Design by:
Christopher Kirk
www.GFSstudio.com

For Sophie June.
May your sweet but short life continue
to have an eternal impact on this earth.

TABLE OF CONTENTS

PREFACE

I was a freshman in high school when the TV show *The Apprentice* first made its way into our homes in 2004. As a teen who wasn't yet old enough to have a job, it was comical to watch Donald Trump sit in his intense boardrooms and say, "You're fired!" I thought, *Is this really how things are like in real life?* Learning that "reality shows" are usually far from reality, I soon realized it was more of a game show.

Sitting here today, Fall 2021, I am shocked to find out there have been over seventy seasons of the show that now spans thirty-three countries. Three more countries—Brazil, Indonesia, and South Africa—are set to release a new season of their version of *The Apprentice* in the months ahead. Maybe the show is so wildly popular because the *reality of* being fired from a job is all too familiar to so many people.

The reality hit me in the Spring of 2017 as a twenty-eight-year-old husband and father of two kids under two. I was in my "dream job" as a pastor that worked primarily with high school students. It was in high school that Jesus changed my life forever. I had a purpose and meaning for living that went beyond getting good grades, excelling in sports, and landing that academic or athletic scholarship to get into the college of my dreams. I wanted to be a youth pastor and work primarily with high school students so I could watch them be forever changed by a personal relationship with Jesus too.

For nearly two years, I worked in this position at my church until that one fateful day when my supervisor and another pastor in the church sat me down and said, "You're not a good fit at this church." I'm not sure which is worse: being told straight up that "you're fired" or having it sugar-coated with nuanced phrases that make you feel like something is wrong with you. Suddenly, I faced a reality I wasn't ready to face.

Trials are a part of life, but I never thought one of the biggest trials I would face would be getting fired from a church. I thought that only happened in big corporations—in the business world—or when you did something morally wrong or, perhaps worse, illegal. Not for being a bad fit! And fired from a church? I never thought the Church, the people Jesus gave up His life for, would be the starting point to the greatest *refined by fire* process in my life.

But as I have come to realize over the years, many pastors and other church staff find themselves in these circumstances too—just as the many others in jobs in every industry who are let go. And some of us have been fired in some difficult, surprising, and hurtful ways. The hardest thing for me was the idea that the Church is supposed to be a shelter in times of need, a place to find hope and healing when you have experienced an unfair tragedy. So where do you turn when you don't find a shelter but a battlefield instead?

Google. Yep, that's right. I turned to Google, like any person does, to figure out what to do in my crisis. I typed:

How to deal with being fired from a church.
My church fired me. Now what?
When the church hurts you because they fired you.
When a pastor is fired.

To my surprise, there were no answers; the results were sparse, mostly non-existent. I found a couple of random blogs but nothing of substance that I could relate to my situation and what I was feeling. I made my search more generic, looking for anything about being fired, and all I found were blogs, subreddits, and advice from financial companies on how to collect unemployment.

I learned churches, and many non-profits, don't pay unemployment tax, which means if you're fired, you can't collect unemployment. Nothing was helpful for the internal carnage. It seemed everything was communicated in a five-step plan that I thought was unrealistic to achieve and didn't deal with the emotions I felt. Where were the resources that could help me process, grieve, be angry, ask hard questions of Jesus and my faith, *and* help me land on my feet because I had a family to take care of financially?

To be fair, I probably didn't stay in that Google search long enough because I found a couple of books written to help people who had recently been fired from a job, though they were usually jobs outside of the church.[1] One interesting find was *Moving*

---

1 Wagner, Megan. 2017. *Fighting Fired with Fire: A Guide to Coping with Job Loss, Rising from the Ashes and Igniting a Career You Love.* CreateSpace Independent Publishing Platform.

On: Surviving the Grief of Forced Termination by Deanna Harrison, written for pastors in 2016.[2] Deanna shares the story of her husband being forced to resign from his role as senior pastor after being at the church for several years. She is now the executive director of Pastors' Hope Network, founded in 2019, which focuses on providing hope and help for pastors and their families who have been fired and are now in transition. I would encourage you to check out her organization and see if it's an organization where you could receive the love and care you and your family need.

Just one book. I found one book. In a culture inundated with hundreds of thousands of books ranging across hundreds of topics, like nutrition, exercise routines, faith, politics, marriage, and sex, I wondered how there could be only one about how to recoup and recover from being fired from a church.

It was just over twenty-four hours after being fired, and I knew I had to put my emotions into words. I spilled my words in my journal and then onto a scribbled, tear-stained paper, then to a typed Word document. Through it all, Jesus helped me make sense of everything for myself and, as I wrote, possibly for others. The irony hit me. For someone who loathed writing any more than twenty pages for the undergraduate and graduate classes he took, shock exploded inside me. Because right away, I sensed Jesus calling me to write this book. The desire in me was so strong, not only to help myself process my pain and grief but also because I had a strong desire to help the next pastor, the next church staff member, the next fired employee have a

2 Harrison, Deanna. 2015. *Moving On*. Book's Mind.

life-giving resource at their disposal. I was ready to be *refined by the fire(d)*.

How This Book Will Help You

First, I want to help those who have or will have to endure the painful reality of being fired, forced to resign, or "mutually agree" to go their separate ways. Because my story unfolded in a church, my goal is to speak primarily to those who share that unfortunate experience. However, there will be many transferable principles you can apply to losing a job outside of the church. As I talk with people in the business world, they resonate with my experience and see how what I learned is helpful to them in their firing.

I want you to work through your brokenness and your pain. As you endure this trial, I hope you will be refined and made stronger in your faith and life, just as God designed.

Second, I want you to leave your church or job well. Most people who are fired do not feel like they should have been fired (a *majority* may even be an understatement). They feel mistreated, sometimes hurt, because someone in a leadership position may have acted horribly against them. Those feelings may be valid, and you may be right—that your boss got it wrong in firing you. But I believe what God wants more than anything else is for you to leave your position with so much grace and mercy that, to your supervisor, your leaders, and in my context, your church, it reflects the grace God shows each of us every day.

Third, I want all employers to read my story and think of how they can be even more gracious, kind, loving, and caring when the tough decision comes to have to fire someone. This book is not about eliminating firings but about how we might become more gracious, empathetic, and clear in the steps leading up to the firing. This book should grow a desire within leadership to care more about their teams than what any individual can produce for their "bottom lines." In the church, specifically, I hope church leaders might see their staff members as the primary people they should focus on in Jesus's call to "make disciples," instead of seeing them as a means to an end or positions to fill to lead a ministry at the church.

Finally, I want to help those in the church who have just lost a beloved church staff member to a firing. The dynamic between our relationship with God and our relationship with the Church can blur quickly when this happens to our pastors or ministry staff. We, too, need the space to grieve, mourn, and be reminded that the Church *is* the hope of the world, even when things feel a little hopeless. I pray that through reading my story and the countless nuggets of wisdom that were imparted to me by the far too many who had experienced being fired or seeing someone fired, we would all be *refined by the fire(d)*. Let's enter "the fired" together as we process our pain, regain our purpose, and persevere through it all so that we come out stronger and more like Jesus on the other side.

INTRODUCTION

Metals are the most valuable commodity in our society. From the monetary worth of gold, silver, and bronze to the steel that holds up almost every tall building, to the brass and copper pipes that allow electricity and water to flow freely through your house, metal is found everywhere. Many kinds are underrated yet vitally important for our day-to-day living. I am thankful that metals go through an intense process of being refined by fire so they can hold immense weight and be a conduit of electricity. When metals go through the fire—hundreds, even thousands of degrees Fahrenheit of fire—their value increases.

In the Bible, the Apostle Peter writes about the Christian faith in this way. "So be truly glad. There is wonderful joy ahead, even though you must endure many trials for a little while. These trials will show that your faith is genuine. It is being tested as fire tests and purifies gold—though your faith is far more precious than mere gold. So when your faith remains strong through many trials, it will bring you much praise and glory and honor on the day when Jesus Christ is revealed to the whole world" (1 Peter 1:6–7, NLT). When our lives are filled with trials, it will allow us to grow our faith, strengthen our character, and become more like Jesus. He endured the greatest trial; He was refined by the hottest of fires, bearing the sins of humanity and overcoming death once and for all for our good and His glory, honor, and praise. Trials are a guarantee in this life, and if you're in a trial-by-fire(d) season, get ready to get stronger, just like Jesus, no matter how hot it gets.

1
THE INITIAL FIRING

On the morning of April 7, 2017, I received a text from my supervisor, asking me if I could have an "advanced meeting" with him and our lead pastor at the campus. An advanced meeting was typically a way for leaders to help staff members grow as productive members of the team and be even better contributors to the church as a whole. I was excited to not only have this scheduled with my supervisor, the executive pastor, but also with the lead campus pastor—the two guys that managed most of our staff.

What happened that afternoon, one week before Easter, ended up being a complete shock. The meeting started with my supervisor saying, "Kyle, over these last couple of months, as we have rolled out our church's new vision and core values, we have had a couple of conversations about how you don't necessarily see eye-to-eye on all the values. I know you've said you are willing to learn them and change, but I just don't see that happening. We don't think this is working out as our church moves forward." I could feel my heart drop right through my stomach. Before we get into the details of the next forty-five minutes of this conversation, let me set some background context.

My Backstory

Almost two years before this meeting, I was hired by a different campus pastor and a different executive pastor of the church to lead the youth ministry. One month into my job, the campus pastor was no longer my supervisor. The executive pastor had been demoted, and a new executive pastor had been promoted. A year later, that new executive pastor was fired (with three other full-time staff quitting in the same month), and my next new supervisor was the long-standing worship pastor . . . now, executive pastor. That's right. In that meeting on April 7, I was sitting in front of my fourth boss in less than two years. Confused and exhausted yet? I sure was!

These changes came with a lot of new expectations, new relationships that had to be forged, and a new understanding I had to reach of what each changed value and priority in ministry had become. When new leaders emerge in any organization, there's a need for the remaining staff to catch their supervisor up about where things stand in the ministry and where things are going. Then there's the supervisor's job to communicate and implement their unique expectations and desires about where the ministry is going. If you have been on either side of this equation, you know this can take some time and be quite challenging. When you have repeated this process four times in a brief span, the challenge becomes . . . well, even more challenging.

The first six months working for my newest supervisor were great—from the beginning of the summer through the middle of the fall of 2016. There was a high level of trust afforded me; there were more church-wide responsibilities given to me on top of my youth ministry responsibilities; there were also some good things happening in the high school ministry. The senior pastor had even praised me in front of our staff because I had shared that through all the transitions the previous year, as well as the many transitions that took place in my first church ministry job, my goals were to remain positive, stay out of the gossip, and focus on what the Lord had for me as the youth pastor.

Toward the end of October, my wife gave birth to our second child. I took two weeks off to be home, and then I came back excited about what was next as we learned how to balance life with two kids under two and my job leading the youth ministry.

During the next couple of months, my supervisor and I began to stray from seeing eye-to-eye on defining "wins" or successes for the high school ministry. Certain events or outreaches that I thought went well were deemed unsuccessful, or at least described as not the way the pastor would have executed the programs. He wanted high numbers of students coming to our church building for a big, energetic event. I programmed events off-site, with a focus on developing relationships between students and between students and their leaders. Neither of us neglected the primary purpose of helping students to know and follow Jesus; we just didn't agree on what that primary strategy should be for these outreach events. It was through this process that my supervisor and I had our first real conversation to clear the air.

It was the day before Christmas Eve. I reminded him I had asked for feedback and mentoring, but I never got it and didn't trust him enough yet to provide it, since he had never shown up to any of my youth group nights to evaluate me. He agreed he needed to show up so that his feedback would be valid, instead of just giving his thoughts after the fact. We also talked about how our ideas of what a win was for high school ministry looked different, and we now needed to clarify what wins were moving forward. I was encouraged by this initial conversation. As I look back, however, maybe I should've pursued the clarity conversation again after the first of the year instead of waiting for him to initiate it. It seemed to have fallen through the cracks.

January came and went with a heavy focus on our high school winter retreat, one that ultimately became a huge win for me, as well as for my supervisor. But I now realize it was a win for different reasons, and the disparity once again showed itself in the annual High School Super Bowl Party the following weekend. For some reason, a super bowl party is one of the most hotly debated events in youth ministry. I've never had a preference—for it or against it—mainly because I always enjoyed the time to connect with students and leaders. After a fun and exhausting winter retreat, I looked forward to that next weekend when a family from our church had offered to cook for and host sixty-plus high schoolers in their home! It was the perfect opportunity to connect with the students again, following up with everyone about what they experienced at the winter retreat. The party went well, or so I thought.

The following Tuesday, our staff went through a full-day training with a church consulting group. This group analyzed data from a test they administered to determine the characteristics of the "Top 400" leaders in the world (from the military, government, ministry, sports, business, and other industries). The way individual reports were generated was by having five to six people, including yourself, look through a list of three hundred words. If you or another person thinks a word describes you, you put a checkmark next to it. Then the group uses their computer wizards to pump out the data from this test. It was all very fascinating and pretty accurate.

On top of all of this, our senior pastor shared how we were trying to refine our staff culture and get everyone aligned with a common vision. With so many transitions over the previous year, he felt it was important to ensure the staff knew who we were as a church so that, as we moved into the summer, we could strategically plan ahead and "hit the ground running" in the fall. I was excited because not only would I gain a greater understanding of how I could be a better leader, but I also assumed there would be greater clarity moving forward about what our church was looking to do. I felt like I could finally align my expectations with my supervisor's about what a win was for the ministry I served.

After this training day, my supervisor and I sat down and looked over the results. We talked about the things I learned and the ways I could grow. That was all helpful, and I was encouraged by it all, but then the conversation shifted. My supervisor explained to me that he had figured out why some of our discussions over the past few months about the events I'd done with the youth group bothered him so much. He told me how disappointed he was to find out we did not have the

Super Bowl party at the church. This was a surprise to me since the two of us, along with the junior high pastor, had talked about this party back in November, *and* he had seen and approved my calendar of events for the winter and spring seasons before Christmas, which included the party's location at the family's home.

He believed, "We are a church that gathers in our place." We have a building; we have a space; we meet consistently every weekend at the same time in the same place, and when we throw the big event, the big party, we bring people "in" that way. That was our church's way! (This was pre-covid.) It seemed to me we were too focused on getting people to show up for church instead of *being* the Church.

But aha! The light bulb went off in my head! It made sense why he'd grown frustrated with me over what seemed like small decisions, even though there'd also been decisions where he had allowed me to make the final call.

At the end of this meeting, he asked me if I was willing to learn how to lead the ministry the "church's way." He further explained how my way of leading ministry differed from the church's, but that we all needed to align our strategies to be on the same page. I nodded my head and shared that I wanted to get clarity on what he was concerned about because, at the end of the day, I know we are all pursuing one primary goal for our church youth ministry: making disciples of students, helping students know Jesus, and following Him.

I was ready to listen. I left that meeting in February feeling hopeful because I'd finally heard some specific direction from my supervisor. Mainly, hold events at the church!

That same month, my supervisor had also asked me to talk with some families in the church whose high school student wasn't attending our youth group gatherings consistently. Though new students and more students were coming to the youth group that year, there were some families with high school students who did not want to get plugged in yet. While talking with these parents, my supervisor wanted me to set up a meeting with all the parents to discuss their ideas together so we could be better learners of how to care for their students. I pursued these conversations with six families. Every one of them appreciated me coming to them and shared their perspectives about their students and our ministry—all of which had to do with their child not connecting with other students or a small group leader. However, none of them had any desire to meet with my supervisor and me in that type of large-group setting with other families. They told me they would feel awkward having a meeting with other parents about something so personal and unique to their child. I reported all of this to the pastor, yet he still wanted me to schedule a meeting with at least a couple of families.

Finally, I got one set of parents to agree to such a meeting, and it was in this meeting that I shared the vision and mission of our ministry with these parents. They were on board with it. We talked, and I felt both sides were heard, and it seemed like practical steps were put in place to help this couple's daughter get more connected. The pastor ended the meeting by thanking them for their time and saying, "There won't be any drastic changes made to the youth group, but we just want to hear from you and learn from you." This meeting took place five days before I was fired from my position.

April 7: Back to the Initial Firing

I was not the right fit for our church's youth ministry. My supervisor affirmed my gifts as a youth pastor, leader, teacher, and shepherd, as well as my love and care for students, leaders, and families. But ultimately, he believed I would thrive in a different environment—not his, not this church.

After a few minutes, I spoke up for the first time. "I don't feel like you have given me a chance to learn our church's way of doing things. You've only recently clarified this for me. We have been going through these things for only two months, and the action items you have told me to do, I have done. In my opinion, two months is too short of a time to evaluate any changes."

In his mind, it had been longer than two months. Even though I had been waiting longer, he had only provided some clarity in February. He believed I'd had plenty of opportunities to change. He had a manila folder filled with examples that "proved" how it was not going to work out, and how ultimately, "I was not teachable . . . unwilling to collaborate with him." He brought up some of the previously mentioned events and how I should've listened to his initial feedback on doing something big at the church. I pushed back, explaining that if there was something he wanted to be done his way, a non-negotiable, he should have mandated it. He should not have given me the option to make the final decision or conduct meetings where the other people in the room agreed with me and then trusted me with the decision. His argument: "We are a church that leads by influence, not mandate." In my mind, in a season of new visioning and aligning staff, there needed to be mandating, not merely suggestions, especially if our jobs depended on whether our "choices" matched the supervisors' opinions. I reiterated that it seemed to me like those were healthy discussions, and at the end of the day, many times over, he still saw "wins" with doing things "my way," even if it wasn't the method he was expecting.

He immediately changed direction and told me I didn't willingly collaborate with him as the other staff did. "Out of all the staff I oversee, you are the one who stops by my office the least to ask me questions."

I explained that every week before I plan out the program for the youth group, I go over the feedback he gave me from the first—and only time—he came to the youth group to evaluate it, at the beginning of January. I showed him how I had implemented his feedback and reminded him of conversations we'd had about how I was doing this consistently.

He then said I wasn't implementing the "big event" nights focused on tons of fun and games with a five-minute message at the end. Our junior high pastor was using them monthly and had garnered a large attendance at his youth group nights.

I reminded him of the two events I held the previous semester and the many more I had planned for the fall and spring of the next year.

He then said he had to force me to do them and that I was unwilling to listen to his suggestions about them. I told him that my only pushback had been that I didn't think it was beneficial to do them once a month but twice a semester for high school students.

As you can see, the conversation was going nowhere. I saw it too . . . and so did the other pastor in the room. So the campus pastor interjected and said, "Do you really want to be in a place where you have to be told the things you need to do?" I told him that for a season, this season, I was willing to learn. I was willing to be stretched out of my comfort zone and adjust because I knew God could grow me and use this time to make me a better leader and pastor. I did not want to be in a place where this was happening all the time, true, but I thought I would be okay for a season.

My supervisor jumped in and told me he couldn't prod me along anymore. He said, "This isn't the place where we can push people along; they need to be on board and moving forward together." He reiterated he had been pushing me along for over six months. It was when he said that I knew there was no use saying another word to save my job. So I asked when they wanted me to be done.

I had less than two months. June 1 would be my last day. I would get through Easter, finish the ministry year (four more nights of youth group), and then have a couple more weeks in the office to wrap up and transition myself out of the church. They would give me one month of severance and have me use my vacation time for the last two weeks of May to get me to July 1 with the severance. (Remember, there was no unemployment, so time was ticking). The conversation ended with my supervisor reiterating that the church and its youth ministry were just not the right fit for me, but that I was a good youth pastor and could thrive in a different church environment. The campus pastor ended our time by praying for me, and I left. I got in my car, with tears filling my eyes and a cloud of shame hovering over my head, feeling like the biggest failure ever.

I pulled into my driveway and saw my two-year-old daughter and my father-in-law in our front yard. My daughter had the biggest smile on her face because this was the first time she was still outside when I pulled in from work. It was like a whole new experience for her, to get to see her daddy step out of his car and run up to him and give him a big hug. She was usually inside, waiting for the garage door to open, which signified Daddy's return home. As she was experiencing something for the first time, I prayed right then that as I experienced being fired for the first time, I could find joy like the joy I saw on her face. I held back tears (having dark sunglasses helped), picked up my daughter, and gave her a big hug and kiss. I greeted my father-in-law, went inside, and went into "Dad" mode.

The Wilderness

My wife, Maria, was in a season where she was experiencing intense back and pelvis pain. Under her doctor's orders, she could not lift more than five pounds. She was not driving—even being in a car caused her discomfort—but she had to get to physical therapy, the chiropractor, and to therapeutic massages. There were five or six appointments every week. So there needed to be someone at our house with her 24/7, including when I wasn't there, to help out with our daughter and five-month-old son. When I was home, I was taking care of two kids and my wife.

When I walked inside, I got my son into his car seat, packed up the car, and the three of us headed to one of her many appointments that week while my daughter stayed at the house with Grandma and Grandpa.

"How was your day, babe?"

I was dreading hearing those words from my wife on our thirty-minute ride to the chiropractor. To my surprise, I didn't cry immediately when I told her I was fired. However, tears flowed from her eyes. And it didn't take long for the liquid pain to fall from my eyes once I reiterated the conversation I had at work.

"How can this be? . . . This is so unfair. You're not a bad youth pastor; you're a great youth pastor." My wife was going from shock to anger, to selflessly loving and encouraging me, all in a span of seconds. I recounted more and more details, then dropped her off for her appointment. Parents of infants and toddlers know the car is your best friend when trying to keep a sleeping child asleep. For her hour-plus appointment, my son and I drove around town, and by God's grace, he slept the entire time, even on the car ride home! This drive gave me a lot of time to think, to cry, to pray, and even to talk to another youth pastor in the area who was mentoring me that year.

My mind raced with questions: How would I tell my students? My leaders? My co-workers? My family? My daughter's second birthday party was the next day . . . how was that supposed to go? What should I do next? Do I look for a youth pastor job somewhere in the area? Do I look to become more of a lead pastor? Do we move somewhere else? Do I stop doing ministry? For a season? *Forever?* Do I just get a "normal" job? Do I need to re-format my resume? Do I need to have two different resumes, one for church jobs and one for "normal" jobs? How would I ever get a job in ministry again if I was fired? Do I go back to school and get my doctorate so I can teach? (That last thought came and went faster than free pizza at youth group). How can I afford a house payment on a home we've lived in for less than a year? Do we get our house ready to sell? Will I join the millions[3] of millennials who have to live in their parents' basements? Will I go bankrupt?

My mind was *all* over the place.

On the way home, my wife calmed my heart and mind a bit, reminding me of the season our family was in: "The Wilderness." As I mentioned before, my wife was having serious back and pelvic issues. It all started with a terrible epidural experience during the birth of our daughter, where they "missed" when sticking the needle into her back. Then the head anesthesiologist came in forty-five minutes later, and on her first try, did it correctly. This experience started my wife on a trajectory of muscle tension and pain that eventually landed us where we were.

Almost two years later, and after a successful natural delivery five months earlier, my wife was finally gaining more strength in her back. It seemed like the end was in sight, and her second labor and delivery seemed to be the natural reset her body needed. She was feeling better but still needed consistent chiropractic care.

At the end of February 2017, about six weeks before my firing, something happened that put Maria in more pain than she had ever been in before. Somehow, her pelvis went out of alignment, causing an incredible amount of physical pain, which significantly affected her function (yes, it hurts as bad as it sounds). So we were in the heat of this crazy season of constant appointments, with zero margin, running on empty, and wondering why she was experiencing this terrible pain every moment of her life. Throughout this season, the women's group at our church was

3 My overly dramatic estimate.

going through a Priscilla Shirer Bible study on the Israelites as they trekked through the wilderness. The study was called "One in a Million."[4]

One main idea we took from this was how God had led the Israelites through the wilderness when there was a much quicker way to get to the Promise Land from Egypt. Yes, the long road was brought on because of their sin, but God had a specific purpose for leading the Israelites the way He did. And for our family, our anthem was that we were learning to become even more dependent on God on our wilderness journey. We were confident God would completely heal my wife, but He was purposefully leading us through this season of long-suffering.

While talking about getting fired, Maria came to believe it was another aspect of our wilderness journey. God was going to do a work in our lives through this difficult process. And time and time again, we reminded each other of this: that instead of praying only for God to heal and remove this hardship from our lives, we needed to lean in toward God and His presence, not running away from how we feel but processing the pain in our hearts and lives. We need to seek Him even more during this trial because He was obviously working out something in our lives. We didn't want to miss out on how He might be making us more like Jesus.

Some Bible verses popped into my head as Maria encouraged me. "When troubles of any kind come your way, consider it an opportunity for great joy. For you know that when your

4 "One In A Million Bible Study | Priscilla Shirer | Lifeway." n.d. www.lifeway.com/en/product-family/one-in-a-million.

faith is tested, your endurance has a chance to grow. So let it grow, for when your endurance is fully developed, you will be perfect and complete, needing nothing" (James 1:2–4, NLT). I wanted to go *Frozen* on it and "let it go," but the Lord had a greater purpose for it, to let it *grow* so we could endure and be made perfect and complete.

I imagine that as James, the half-brother of Jesus, was writing this to the new Christians who had scattered from Jerusalem because of the intense religious persecution, he was thinking, "Twelve tribes—new Christians—this is James speaking: I know we are afraid and scattered right now after Stephen's brutal murder at the hands of the Jewish religious leaders; I know we are missing the comforts of being together in Jerusalem and hearing Peter preach to us the 'rich food' from the Old Testament that points to Jesus; I know the threat of the Roman Empire and the Jewish leaders, namely the Pharisees, is scary; but I urge you, stay in it! God is working, and He will be faithful and make us more like Jesus. So find all of this to be a great joy because God is making us more like Jesus!"

So I prayed:

> *OK, Jesus, I'm leaning in. I am going through this, and I am expecting that as we journey through the wilderness, you will make me more like You. And if I am truly sold out with devoting my life to sharing my hope in You with those around me, I better be able to stick with it through the wilderness. No more just teaching from James 1. It's time to put my money where my mouth is and persevere.*

Little did I know this would be one of the hardest, most difficult decisions I would make in my life as a follower of Jesus. But this was not something I had to deal with on my own. Yes, my wife and family were going to be there, but I had to be proactive in this process and seek help right away. I knew someone specific who could understand my situation and help me process things right away: my youth pastor.

About eight years before that fateful day, April 7, 2017, my youth pastor, mentor, and role model had taken a position at a church in California as a high school pastor. He'd packed up his family from the Midwest and headed west. Fifty-three days later, he was told to pack up his books, clear out his office, and leave the church. No forty-five-minute conversation. No exit interview. He just had to leave. He re-packed his family and drove the U-Haul back to the Midwest.

After bouncing around in a couple of different jobs, he had secured a great position as a pastor and had been in the role for a few years. I texted him that night, and we talked for over an hour the next day. Honestly, he did a lot more listening than talking. I wanted to soak in his wisdom like I had been doing since I was fifteen years old (I was now twenty-eight). I knew his experience was "worse" than mine and that he had worked through so much of the hurt already. I was hoping to get the million-dollar answers, but he just kept asking me questions.

After telling him the details of the story, he asked me different things like, "What are *your* blind spots? What are the truths *you* can take away from what your supervisor said about *you*? What does this reveal about *your* heart for ministry and for

Jesus? How can *you* show grace and love because love covers a multitude of sins? How can *you* leave well?"

I wasn't ready for this conversation. I didn't want to hear about all these things *I* needed to do; I just wanted someone who would let me vent, tell me I was right, confirm for me that my supervisor was wrong, and say everything would be just fine in the end. He did share for about ten minutes at the end of our conversation and reaffirmed this Scripture for me: "And we know that for those who love God all things work together for good, for those who are called according to his purpose" (Romans 8:28, NLT). He was less concerned about my firing while still being empathetic and compassionate toward me. He was more concerned about me being more like Jesus and treating everyone, especially my supervisor, like Jesus would: full of grace and forgiveness. The last thing he asked me to do was to journal; journal everything. Journal answers to the questions he was asking me. Journal what God was teaching me through his Word. Journal my conversations with my wife and with others. Journal as much as possible during this time because when you get pen to paper, it allows you to fully lean into what God wants you to hear.

And journal I did. In fact, journaling through that process is what created the passion in me to write this book and helped me remember and articulate my experiences and emotions accurately.

The Commonality

I don't know the statistics of pastors who are fired or forced to resign from their jobs for reasons not associated with moral failures or illegal activity, but I know it's a lot . . . too much. The US

Bureau of Labor Statistics produces a monthly report of hiring, firings, and unemployment rates. For the last six months of 2022, well over one million people were laid off or fired per month.[5] A 2012 study published in the Review of Religious Research found that about one in three pastors have or will face a forced termination in their ministry careers.[6]

I don't know the percentage of people who are fired for reasons that are not illegal or immoral, but my guess is most of those people believed they were in their dream job one day, and by the end of that same day, they were not. There is something clearly wrong, but instead of pointing fingers at the system, the individual leaders, or the employees, let's first start with ourselves.

We are a bunch of broken people, trying to work for and lead other broken people. In the church world, we are a bunch of broken pastors, trying to lead broken people to know Jesus and make Him known in our world. Yet, it is in this brokenness that God wants us to stay and persevere because it is in this brokenness that God can grow us exactly how He wants to grow us. It reminds me of the prophet Isaiah and his prophetic word about the Father's plan for His Son, Jesus: "But it was the Lord's good plan to crush him and cause him grief" (Isaiah 53:10, NLT).

Yes, this verse is all about God's plan of saving the world through Jesus's death and resurrection, but I couldn't help but resonate with this verse as I first thought about my firing. I think there is something to reflecting on how God was most glori-

---

5 "Economic News Release: Job Openings and Labor Turnover Summary." U.S. Bureau of Labor and Statistics, Feb 1, 2023. www.bls.gov/news.release/jolts.nr0.htm

6 "Forced Termination on American Clergy: Its Effects and Connection to Negative Well-Being." Marcus Tanner, Anisa Zvonkovic, and Charlie Adams. March 2012.

fied in His Son's obedience to the suffering He experienced on the cross. It was a part of God's good plan for our salvation. In Jesus's greatest pain and hardest trial, He and the Father were most glorified. This led me to believe that God was not surprised by my firing, even allowed my firing, and had specific ways He wanted to grow, refine, and make me more like Jesus through this particular trial. But I had to lean into processing, persevering, and regaining my purpose to see the good in His plan.

In Jesus's greatest pain and hardest trial, He and the Father were most glorified.

I wholeheartedly believe the same is true for you! In the chapters ahead, as I further unfold my story, you will see the ideas of processing pain, regaining purpose, and persevering woven throughout the pages of my story. It is important that you commit today to use this threefold lens to view your firing as you step into your refined by the fire(d) season. If you're there right now or need to reflect on that time in your life when you experienced a firing, the first step I would encourage you to do is to begin journaling or taking notes—today! Use the framework of processing pain, regaining purpose, and persevering to guide your writing. What does this look like?

Processing Pain

As a follower of Jesus, I started by journaling what I learned from the Bible and hearing from God in prayer. For the readers who share my Christian faith, that is where you begin: journal what you sense Jesus is revealing to you through His Word and in prayer. If you're not comfortable reading the Bible or praying because you share a different faith, I would still encourage you to reflect on some of the Bible verses or prayers I include, ones you will see scattered throughout this book. As I shared earlier, there is something about the humble life of Jesus that is so relevant to being fired from a job. He understands pain and suffering on a different level, one that can help us on our worst days.

After that, journal about your conversations with co-workers, family members, friends, and even your interactions with your leader. Not only should you do this for your emotional and mental sanity, but also because I truly believe this will help reveal what God is trying to teach you in your firing, in your wilderness season.

The Promise Land seems very, very far away at this point, but don't worry; there are four books of the Bible that cover forty years of the Israelites' journey through the wilderness. So get ready to write and be thankful you aren't carving it into stone tablets like Moses. We will get into some of the most self-revealing times in my life, times when God really challenged and changed my heart to give me a new heart for Him and for others. And my prayer is that as you read this book and do your own journaling, He will do the same for you.

Regain Purpose

We live in a culture where our job ends up being one of the main ways we find identity, purpose, and meaning. Think back to the last conversation you had with someone you were meeting for the first time. What are those first couple of questions you asked or were asked: your name, maybe where you live, and at some point, "What do you do?" Work is a good thing. It's something God created in the beginning, and it is something we will do in eternity, but it's not our identity. Unfortunately, our jobs have become our identities; even our kids are taught from a very young age that school is about the progression of getting an education that will get them into the college that will help them answer the question, "What do you want to do when you grow up?" In the church world, I am most often introduced as "Pastor Kyle." Doctors understand this phenomenon too—how your job redefines your name, your identity, and your purpose in life.

Let me be clear: ***your job is not your identity; it is not your purpose in life. You have a greater purpose in life than what you do from nine to five (or any other shift of work)!*** From my Christian perspective, it's about living a life as a child of God and pointing people to the new life Jesus has for them. No matter your religious beliefs, losing your job helps you see that you still exist as a human. You have an identity and purpose outside of your career. So as you process the immense pain of losing your job, you will begin to see across the pages of your journal your thoughts and feelings, which will help you regain your purpose in life, and it is not, nor has ever been, dependent on your job.

Persevere

This work is hard. Some days, it's even harder than being fired in the first place. While you process the pain of being fired, it may bring up past hurts, wounds, and unhealthy patterns of thinking (e.g., your job is your identity). These are thoughts and emotions—maybe lies—you need to feel, work through, and grow from in the future. You may realize that your firing from ten years ago or going through multiple firings or seeing someone else getting fired brings up feelings and emotions you haven't dealt with yet. It is easy to give up on the process and push away the feelings, bury them, and try to move on as quickly as possible. I think we can all agree that is not a strategy for growth. This is true whether you are at the beginning of a firing or experienced a firing years ago. You will carry these pains, identity issues, and anything else with you into your next job, next church, next pastorate, and next relationship. It is better to do the work now so that when those thoughts or feelings arise later, you have already done the hard work to persevere and handle them in an emotionally and spiritually healthy manner. As you will see in my story, the pain and identity issues still come up, but I can consistently go back to the work I did early on in the process to help me move forward when the grief, sorrow, or struggles show up in the forefront of my mind. Stay the course, or, if the firing happened a while ago, jump back in and do the hard work now. It will be worth it in the end.

Ready to begin? Let's move on together in the refined by fire(d) process.

2

PROCESSING THE PAINFUL REALITY OF PRIDE

When I left that meeting on Friday, I was told I did not have to be at church on Sunday morning. However, I still had to lead the youth group gathering that Sunday night without mentioning this to anyone within the church.

Saturday was the day of my daughter's second birthday party. This was also the day I had my first conversation with my youth pastor who gave me the advice to journal and look at how God wanted to work inside me instead of being angry and sad about my external circumstances. Don't worry, I will come back to the anger and sadness in upcoming chapters. I will also get back to the interactions I had with family at the birthday party and the students and leaders at youth group in the next chapter, but I first want to share what happened on Sunday afternoon before youth group. The first part happened while I was at home journaling; the second, while I was at church preparing for youth group.

I began the journaling process by replaying the conversation I had on Friday to see if I could identify any of my blind spots. It felt nearly impossible to do because I was still angry, and I still didn't agree with anything my supervisor had said. So I prayed, and specifically, I was led to pray to help prepare my heart and mind for youth group. I knew the night would be difficult since I couldn't share with anyone what had happened, but that was the only prayer that came to mind. No prayers about my blind spots, no revelation about how I was wrong and he was right . . . nothing. I read some Scripture . . . nothing. I was confused by the silence, but I kept asking God for something (anything!). All I heard was "Prepare for tonight." That was it.

On Sunday nights, I am the only staff member in the church building. Our church building is a renovated, four-story office building with our student space on the third floor and all of our administrative offices on the fourth floor. On the fourth floor, there is a big room where our printer sits. From that room, you can see the majority of the staff offices, including my supervisor's office. On that particular Sunday, his office door was wide open. From my vantage point, I also noted the manila folder he had held in his hand forty-eight hours earlier, the one with his notes of the reasons he fired me. He had said he did not want to go through any of the notes, though we had covered a few. At that moment, I knew I wanted to cover them all. I knew that if I was going to fully heal, learn, and grow, I had to see it all, hear it all, or, in this case, read it all. So I walked into his office, took the three pages from inside the folder, made a copy of them, and put the notes back in his folder. No one would ever know but Jesus and me . . .

You may be thinking, "This is what God was telling you to prepare for, a heist of confidential information, to be the Christian version of Jason Bourne!" I don't think so, even though I wish I could be Jason Bourne. I shouldn't have grabbed the notes, and I probably did violate some level of trust. As I reflect on it, knowing what I know now, I didn't need those notes on that night. However, they led me to have an honest conversation with God, which allowed me to process my pain.

At first, I had to fight the feeling of being so mad these things were on paper, so mad these things were never shared with me in this detail, and ultimately, so mad these small things (in my perspective) were why I had been fired. But the Lord used the notes to bring healing and freedom to my heart and soul.

I read through them once before youth group but had to put them down so I wouldn't dwell on them and ruin my attitude for the rest of the night.

I should clarify something: I do not encourage taking notes from your supervisor . . . or taking anything that is not yours. I am not one that lives by the mantra, "Don't get permission first but ask for forgiveness later." I acted as a complete hypocrite in that moment of weakness.

While you can clearly discern the sin of hypocrisy in my heart, let's look at the blind spots I had as well. In my supervisor's notes, there were three main ideas I took away after spending most of my Sunday night and into Monday reading, praying, and reflecting on the stolen information.

1. There was a lack of willingness on my part to collaborate with my supervising pastor.

I really struggled with this concept because, for the longest time, I had perceived myself, and thought others had perceived me, as a "learner." I was never the kind of person who thought he knew everything or had the mindset of "my way or the highway." Yet, I began to see why my supervisor felt this way. When I was first hired, the junior high pastor and I were given the "keys to the car" of the student ministry and told to drive! The quotation marks came from our three previous supervisors; this was even a part of their "pitch" to us during our interview process. But now, with my fourth supervisor, we seemed to be back in Driver's Ed.

Was it fair? It doesn't matter because that was my reality, and I didn't realize this until after I was fired. When my supervisor gave me suggestions, more times than not, I just explained why I was still going to do it my way. Those instances I shared in the previous chapter were the ones listed in his notes. Even now, as I write this, I still think my ideas were better (but no, I don't struggle with the "my way or the highway mindset" . . . or maybe I do!). Even if I am a truly collaborative person, he perceived me differently based on our interactions. I needed to be more willing to listen, ask clarifying questions, and sometimes just do what my supervisor asked me to do.

Another thing I realized is that the things my supervisor listed were not "make or break" issues for me for leading student ministry. They would still have been hard to implement because, from my perspective, I was being told how to drive the car of student ministry by someone who had little experience in leading student ministries. In church ministry, worship ministry, and leading staff, my supervising pastor was absolutely qualified—and extremely gifted. But with student ministry? Not so much. Admittedly, it's hard being told how to drive by someone who has little knowledge of driving when you've been driving for ten years as the "paid expert." But does my experience, blurred by my arrogance, give me the right to dismiss everything? Absolutely not, and I should have realized that in these small matters, I could have conceded instead of giving every reason why my way was best for the ministry.

In the end, was I willing to collaborate? Not as much as I thought I was. I partnered or acquiesced in the things where I thought my supervisor was the expert, like planning and programming a service. He had been a worship pastor for ten years, so planning out the flow of teaching, music, transitions, announcements, and creative elements was his world. And in these instances, I did listen, took notes, and implemented his suggestions willingly. But in the areas I thought he was not the expert, I went with not only what I thought, but with what other youth ministry experts were saying and doing. I used their philosophies against my supervisor too. Was this right? Yes, and no.

There were times when I thought his lack of youth ministry experience showed, but in other areas, even if I disagreed, I should have gone with his suggestions at the beginning of our working relationship to build trust and lay a foundation of mutual respect.

One of my supervisor's issues with me was that I would only do what he asked if I was "forced" to do it. I know I thought I was in a season where he needed to be crystal clear on things so I would do things the church's way, but it revealed that my default was still to trust myself and my experience over taking suggestions from those in authority over me. Once again, most people who know me would not say I carry a huge "badge of pride" in my approach to ministry, but even a small dose of pride needs to be stomped out and destroyed. That was what the Lord was showing me. Even a hint of pride needs to be weeded out for us to be like Jesus. Maybe if Jesus would've continued his analogy of cutting off limbs when dealing with lust in Matthew 5, he would've said something like ". . . even if there is a hint of pride in your brain, it is like being the most arrogant dictator in the world. So cut off the part of your brain that houses pride because it is better to have half a brain than a full brain with pride hiding inside it." Even if Jesus didn't say that in the Sermon on the Mount, He was saying this to me through His Spirit. My pride needed to be put to death. It hurt to see that kind of arrogance in me, but it was there. And the Lord was doing his refining work in me to make me more like Jesus, the humble servant.

Even if there is a hint of pride in your brain, it is like being the most arrogant dictator in the world. So cut off the part of your brain that houses pride because it is better to have half a brain than a full brain with pride hiding inside it.

Practical Steps for Collaboration

From this revelation, I began to build a better framework for collaborating with those around me." First, I learned I can go the extra mile by asking clarifying questions to see how strong the suggestion or passionate the idea is that I receive from anyone. Not just from a supervisor, but also from volunteers, internal or external leaders, co-workers, and others. One way I've heard a pastor share this concept is by asking, "Is this a soft opinion [suggestion] or a hard opinion [command]?"

Second, I can ask the "why" question again, before sharing my "expert" opinion on why I think I am right and my way is best. I can hear the person's heart through their answer, the reason they feel strongly or maybe not so strongly about any aspect of my job or the organization before sharing my perspective, explaining why I believe my way is the better option or why I don't fully agree with them.

Third, I can validate what they say by repeating their general idea and seeing some aspect of their idea as positive, even if in my heart, I still disagree with the big picture.

Finally, I can be clear that I haven't made a final decision and want to revisit the two sides soon, before finalizing anything. Even if the decision needs to be made that day, I can give myself and the other person some time—even if just an hour—to step away from it (and the emotion) before coming back and finalizing the decision.

I think of James, the half-brother of Jesus. If he was writing a manual on conflict resolution in the workplace, he would likely footnote his words from his epistle that read, "Be quick to listen and slow to speak" (James 1:19, NIV). I realized I needed to apply this directive when receiving a suggestion too. I never want to be the guy who is not a team player. I prided myself in being called a great team player throughout my life to this point, but if one person doesn't see this in me, then I need to humble myself and through the power of the Spirit, work on collaborating willingly with my team, my leaders, my supervisors, and anyone else in ministry.

Do you see that in yourself as well? Maybe pride, even if it lives in the tiniest amount in your heart or brain, will be one of the first and primary things that will go through the refining fire(d).

2. My "philosophy of ministry" didn't fully align with the church's.

This one was not necessarily news to me since we had this discussion two months before I was fired, but I had missed the significance of our difference in opinions. One thing he wrote in his notes is that I told him "I got it" or "I understand," but I really didn't get it. I didn't understand what he wanted me to do. Part of the reason for this was that he was unclear about his expectations, and part of it was that I didn't go the additional mile to understand. Therefore, he was right: at times, I didn't get it.

My focus on ministry was to build relationships with the core leaders and students to equip them to be on mission—not only in youth group but also in their communities, schools, and homes. My supervisor wanted my primary focus to be on drawing students *in* to our youth group so that my core team could carry out the work of the ministry. They seem similar, except I didn't place as high a value on the programming or big outreach events that brought students in like my supervisor did. That was a low value for me because the most important thing, in my mind, was building the team to be on mission, *out* in the world.

He was not against the mission, but he didn't want that to be my main focus since the best way to reach those lost students, in his opinion, was to draw them in with an attractive program. Once again, I don't think either of us would disagree about the importance of a solid youth ministry night and the focus on discipleship that leads to being on mission, but the disagreement came on what should a youth pastor spend their primary time on throughout the week. Neither of us was anti-big events or anti-small groups or pro-individual mentoring, but a youth pastor's primary focus was the sticking point—the place we didn't see eye to eye. And I missed it. I didn't understand that this was a big difference from the way the church wanted to operate and what the church wanted from its ministry.

Now, whether I agree (or you agree) with the strategy difference, what I needed to realize, once again, was how to ask the extra questions to ensure I was in alignment with my supervisor. My vision was to create an environment where small groups were the most important part of the youth group night, and he wanted the most important thing to be a compelling large-scale event with a great flow of teaching, music, and fun games. I finally understood this *after* I was fired.

Practical Steps for Aligning Philosophies

So what can I, or you, do in the future? One thought would be to have these conversations about philosophies of ministry before stepping into the next ministry position. I definitely missed these differences when I was hired and even in my first year of work. Granted, with three different supervisors before this one—I could have been and most likely was—on the same page with those previous supervisors.

In this firing process, someone told me, "Church leaders can't necessarily tell you what they want, but they are really good at telling you what they don't want." It's like when I ask my wife where she wants to go for dinner. I have to give a few suggestions that get denied before we reach her choice of where she wants to eat.

So how do you and I take this approach when working with a supervisor or group of church leaders? The answer is to have a few different ideas to bring to the table and *expect* that all will be critiqued and some will be shot down. Don't give options to the question, "What do you value the most for the youth ministry?" Instead, frame it in this way (this applies to youth ministry): "I want to do a big event once a month where I only share the Gospel and play a ton of fun games. What do you think about that?" Or "I think we should focus primarily on small groups for our program every Sunday night." Or "I prefer to meet in homes twice a month instead of at the church . . ." The list can go on and on. From their responses, you can gauge what the leadership values most by what they like or don't like, affirm or don't affirm.

If I would've taken this approach with my supervisor earlier, had I taken the initiative to do this, it would have brought so much clarity to what he valued most for my work and the youth ministry.

3. My sense of urgency was viewed as too low for my supervisor.

When the infamous consulting group came to our church a couple of months prior to my firing, one of the leadership characteristics they measured was our "sense of urgency." This quantifies a person's inner drive, self-will, the "go and get it done" attitude, or the "see the problem, solve the problem" mentality. If it's rated high, it means you don't need anyone to tell you to do something; you will already be accomplishing it before someone says it needs to be done. On a scale of one to ten, one being "no sense of urgency" and ten being "the highest sense of urgency," the consulting group's results showed that top leaders fall in a range between 8.5 and 9.25. I rated an 8.25; my supervisor was at 9.5.

In my mind, I had a fairly high sense of urgency, but I will be the first to admit that I don't get a huge sense of satisfaction from completing tasks. From my 8.25 perspective, I thought my supervisor needed to "take a chill pill." ☺

When I see a need, I go all out in accomplishing it, but if it is not a priority in my mind, I don't have that same kind of urgency to complete it. This doesn't mean I neglect small tasks. I thrive on completing honey-do lists for my wife; I pride myself on getting my kids ready to go to church or school in the morning. I see those as valuable things.

So a sense of urgency is there, but my supervisor didn't see it. Why? Because I didn't see the need to pursue some of the things he wanted to see accomplished in the ministry. The things he wanted to be done were not a high priority in my mind. I will flesh this out later, as more time and conversations brought to light his perspective regarding my lack of urgency. But I realized that what was a "sense of urgency" issue for my supervisor was in reality a "sense of purpose" issue for me.

Killing Pride

Those first few days were eye-opening for me as the Lord revealed these three blind spots. Within them, there was one common thread: pride. I thought I knew more than my supervisor because I had the experience and had led successful youth ministries in the past. Things were going well, and God was moving in these students' lives. I knew the more I kept focusing on discipleship, relationships, and building up leaders, the more we would see God do some amazing things. That had to be my priority. There's a lot of *I*s in these last few sentences—five to be exact. God was really tearing away any ounce of pride in my heart.

James 4:6 details what God thinks about pride. He opposes those who are prideful. In my time as a "successful" youth pastor, pride grew bigger and bigger in my heart, and I was blind to that growth. God wanted nothing to do with my pride; He opposed it completely. I needed to see this and let Him kill the pride in my life—daily.

Whether you are doing the firing or being fired, pride is something that can easily creep into your heart as you serve in ministry. Satan will do whatever he can to sneak pride into our minds and hearts to get us off track from pursuing humility. Remember, Satan's the author of pride; it's pride that caused him to be cast out of Heaven. It's one of his best tactics to destroy the work God wants to do in and through us all. So my prayer is that you would examine your heart in any conversation, during any disagreement, and determine your motivation. More times than not, there are going to be many Holy Spirit-driven motivations to move forward with ideas, programs, and purposes in ministry.

But as the battle with sin wages war inside of us, pride can creep into our ministry pursuits. Seek understanding from one another; push aside selfish agendas and be willing to listen and try something new, even if it doesn't make sense from your experience.

God opposes the proud but gives grace to the humble, and we are all in desperate need of God's grace. Don't allow the enemy to gain any foothold in your heart. Pursue humility and put to death any trace of pride in your heart. Whatever part of the refining process you find yourself in, take a moment now and ask God to reveal any pride that was or is still in your heart. Confess it to Him and receive the grace that He freely offers when the proud humble themselves before Him.

That day, as I reflected on my supervisor's notes, pride was destroyed in my heart. It was clear to me that God's word for me to "prepare" while I was at home before youth group was necessary so I would have an open mind to the hard truths I uncovered. I needed to open my heart to the fact I harbored pride that had to be exposed.

A Note to Leaders

A pastor once told me that a yearly performance review should never come with surprises. Because you have worked diligently in meeting consistently with your staff, pointing out things that need to be corrected or changed, and affirming things that are done well, the "performance review" is more of a recap of the year. If there is something your staff member needs to work on, they should've had several meetings with you, addressing the issue, as well as communicating solutions for resolving the challenges.

In the same way, a firing should not come as a surprise unless, of course, there is a moral or legal failure. It was ironic that a few months before my firing, we had spent a couple of days going through the consulting firm's six-step process on how to manage, train, and lead volunteers, especially ones who weren't "getting the job done." But none of this was laid out for me.

Leaders, a decision to fire someone should never be made alone. Ideally, you would consult other leaders in your church when thinking through this type of decision, but what I also mean by alone is that your staff member needs to be a part of this process too! There should be multiple conversations leading up to this final decision, conversations in which you clearly communicate something along the lines of, "Hey, if you can't do this or you keep doing this after talking through this multiple times, then our next step will look at how you can transition out of this job." A seemingly harsh truth like this is taken with more love and respect by your staff member when you have put in the extra effort to listen to them, share your concerns with them, help them work on solutions, and honestly evaluate their progress.

3

WASH, RINSE, REPEAT

Identity. Reputation. These were two words I gained a greater understanding of in the first three weeks after being fired. It started the day after my firing, that Saturday, April 8. We were having family over to our house to celebrate our daughter's second birthday.

I struggled with what I was going to tell my parents. My in-laws. My siblings. These were people that had known my wife and me for a very long time. In that long time, we had experienced great "success" in whatever we did. My wife and I had undergraduate degrees and achieved high honors in college; my wife didn't even get an *A-* in college, just *A*s. I completed a Master of Divinity program in three years while working full-time as a youth pastor, with top honors as well. Our church experiences had always been positive; we were well-liked by many and had made a significant impact on students' and families' lives in our six-year-long ministry together as a married couple and even in the four years before that—while dating throughout college.

It felt like that day, a day that should be focused on joy and celebration, would have this black cloud of shame hovering over our heads. I had failed as a youth pastor. My wife, still feeling the negative effects of her injury, felt like she couldn't live up to the high standard of being a mother. Our identities as great people in ministry and great parents—and our reputations—seemed to have evaporated. That Saturday, we knew we had to share what had happened with those closest to us.

I was physically sick that day, like throwing-up sick. I couldn't hold anything down. It was probably a mix of emotions and stress from the day before, along with a flu bug that was going around.

As the time approached, I didn't know what words would come out of my mouth. I didn't know what emotions would come out in my tone and on my face. I didn't know how our family would react. I didn't know anything, and that was scary. I was much more comfortable controlling what people thought about me by living a life that portrayed continual "success" (Enneagram 3, anyone?).

What I didn't yet know was the Lord was ready to flip that idea upside down in the most radical of ways. He was ready to give me His identity and His reputation. He was about to help me cast my old ideas far, far away and exchange them for His will.

My wife suggested I tell my parents first since they would be at our house earlier to help prepare for the party. The two people who, from the time I was born, had been praying that God would make me a "leader" (Dad's prayer) and a "pastor" (Mom's prayer). They would be the first to learn how I had failed their prayers. I remember lying on our couch in the family room while my parents were prepping food in the kitchen. Without giving them eye contact, and instead looking straight at the ceiling, I muttered the words, "Mom, Dad, I got fired yesterday from my job."

Silence. Not even the proverbial crickets were chirping. It was a good thirty seconds of stillness before I finally sat up and looked over to see their reactions. Their heads were down as they continued to prepare food. Tears had formed in their eyes. When I sat up and saw that, the tears flowed from mine. I told them more about why I was fired, the "small" reasons (I hadn't gone all Jason Bourne with the notes yet. That would be the next day), and how I was confused and still in shock from it all.

The practical side of my parents kicked in pretty quickly after that. "When is your last day? Do you get severance? How long before others will know?"

Then it was, "We can help financially; don't worry about that. We can help."

My parents were servants to their cores. They loved to help hurting people by serving them, meeting their specific needs. And needs can be best met by them when the details of those needs are specifically stated. Why am I going into the specifics of this conversation with them? Because people will care for you in crisis in the same ways they normally care for others. That is what's most comfortable for them.

Because people will care for you in crisis in the same ways they normally care for others. That is what's most comfortable for them.

My in-laws—one a teacher, one a professional counselor—were quick to speak kind words of encouragement when I told them later that day. They were quick to remind me of God's faithfulness, God's sovereignty, and God's plan for our lives. For a living, they teach, encourage, and help those in need, so in a crisis, they go to their default. Encouragement.

My sister offered a big, tearful embrace, the same type of embrace I gave her when a year and a half before she had experienced a pregnancy loss.

All of those different expressions of care encompassed the first step of God rewiring my thinking on *identity* and *reputation* to regain my purpose in life. My family didn't care what I did, how "successful" I was, or even why the firing happened. I knew that on some level, but after that day, I experienced it. They loved me and wanted to care for me, for Maria, and for my kids in the ways that they felt most equipped and most comfortable doing. I was a part of their family. Their love was unconditional, and that was definitely not going to change on April 8. And it was for sure not going to take away from celebrating my daughter's birthday!

My family's care was a great reminder of how God wanted to care for me. Even though identity in Christ was something I had taught time and time (and time) again, I needed to get my identity *re*aligned with Christ. I dwelled on Paul's words in Philippians: "For to me, to live is Christ . . ." (Philippians 1:21a, NIV). What good is my life if I don't chase Jesus in every aspect of my life? What good is my life, your life, if those who know us see more of us than Jesus?

Identity Crisis

When someone goes into full-time ministry, they never intend to have their identity and purpose built upon their success. But it is far too easy for our personal success to overshadow His glory. Maybe we see this more in the American Church (I don't have any statistics to back this up. It's just my experience.) Because of our capitalistic business model, when we promote our message or product and get a good return on the investment (more people, more dollars, more followers, more views, more anything), then we think *we* are doing things well. But *we* get too focused on ourselves and promote *me* over *He*. Our identity is less about Jesus and more about how the product of Jesus is helping us accomplish our goals. When people know us, like us, appreciate us, and follow us, before we know it, we are more concerned about *me* over *He*.

My identity, my purpose, was slowly creeping toward being successful in ministry over being a child of God. My reputation of being successful and likable was overshadowing being an ambassador for Christ. God wanted no part of this false identity and a false sense of reputation for me. He wanted to rip it completely away. Thankfully, this was like a slow, Band-Aid rip. The pain was hard, but I'm so glad it started with the love and care He showed me through my family that day.

I believe God wants to do that for everyone in ministry. When you get fired, it is a great time to evaluate your heart and determine how you define your identity and reputation. If there is even an ounce of false identity and reputation, ask God to take it away. It's not worth it to hold on to whatever you have left of this lie. Bring that dark falsehood into the light and let God's Spirit remove any guilt, shame, and false narrative that's hindering you from finding your identity in Christ alone.

The process won't happen overnight; you will need to daily remind yourself of this truth: *I am a child of God, and I live my life to point people to Jesus.* That's how to live your best life. Nothing short of that will satisfy you. Wash, rinse, repeat. Tell it to yourself over and over again! I thank God He revealed this to me when He did, and it allowed me to enter this next phase of being more like Jesus: *how to live and talk above reproach.*

(Almost) Above Reproach

Now back to Jason Bourne Sunday.

Besides making a copy of my supervisor's notes, youth group still had to go on. Thankfully, I did not have to teach. I had already scheduled a volunteer to do that night's teaching months in advance. I think I would have cried throughout my entire message if I had to speak. I knew going into that night, I could not share anything with anyone because that was what the pastors asked of me. Would it be hard to interact with leaders and students without tearing up? Yes. Would my being fired be on my mind for the entire night? Probably. I knew I couldn't control this situation being in the forefront of my mind, but I could control how I would interact with those around me.

Before the night started, I asked myself, *How did Jesus act during immense inner turmoil?* The answer: He never stopped praying about it. When faced with the enormity of bearing the punishment for all of humanity's sins, He spent time alone with the Father. And then, when put on trial, He didn't defend himself.

I knew the battle within my heart and mind would be great, so I looked to model Jesus by praying silently and fervently throughout the night. I would not bring it up, not make any snide or snarky comments to leaders, and be a positive, encouraging light to all. On many youth group nights, it was easy to do the latter, but unfortunately, the prayer part was the least on my mind. I had the propensity to become "super youth pastor" and do things through my own strength, depending on my gifts and personality. That night, I knew it would have to be different. But not just that night. I needed to shift my mindset, to act like Jesus in thought and word.

I made it through the night pretty well, trying to keep my mind on my students and not on my present circumstances. I owed it to them to love them well this next month because I would end up being their fourth youth pastor in five years. They needed to be reminded of God's love and His goodness, no matter what life threw at them. They needed to see me, their youth pastor, talk and act in a way that was positive and encouraging, even though turmoil was present inside. They would have time later, when the truth was revealed, to see me mourn. But not yet, so I couldn't show that to them. I think this was something that remained in mind over the next month, as some people found out and others didn't. I knew I couldn't sulk or be cynical or grumpy around others who had no idea what had happened yet.

Once again, in the most intense turmoil Jesus faced, He continued to humbly and graciously love and care for His disciples. It was not a sob fest at the Last Supper—maybe a confusion fest because the disciples didn't get the whole dying and rising from the dead thing. But not a sob fest. Jesus not only completed His earthly mission, but He also did it with an attitude that allowed

His disciples and closest family and friends to stay on mission. Was there mourning soon after His death happened? Absolutely! And it wasn't until His resurrection from the dead that things changed in their hearts and attitudes. But I knew I wasn't close to "death," so I couldn't act like it. I had to take on the attitude of Jesus and keep loving and caring for people, even though they were in the dark about the darkness I was in.

This concept trickled into every encounter with anyone in my church family: the other staff, the families, and the students. This was hard, but the Lord was confirming this idea through conversations with people in my church.

God at the Dinner Table

The next day, my family had dinner plans with a family from our church. They had been at this church for almost ten years and were invested in the life of the church. They were a bit older than us, with kids a few years older than our kids, but in a similar phase of life. Usually, there are times during these dinners with people in your church when they ask you how things are going at church. I was nervous about this inevitable question. I hoped and prayed all night it wouldn't come, but unfortunately it did.

I gave a generic answer at first, but then the husband asked how I was doing through all the changes within the staff. I almost laughed out loud—no joke. If I would've had a sip of my drink in my mouth at that moment, I would've sprayed it across the room.

Then he got even more specific. The husband mentioned my former supervisor (fired nine months before me) and my current supervisor. He talked about how the former pastor seemed to have been a "micro-manager" (his words, not mine) and wondered how my relationship was with both of them. I paused.

Then I somehow answered. "All supervisors may come off as micro-managing in certain parts of the job because those are the parts they are most passionate about." So contrary to my friends' belief, I shared honestly that there were things both of them were very "passionate" about in youth ministry. I knew that was as much as I could say because I did not want to go into slander; I didn't want to vent, or as some Christians who want to make themselves feel better call it "sharing prayer requests." He agreed with my perspective and recalled a situation like that in his work. I thought I had done it—avoided any more conversation and could move on—though if I'm honest, deep down inside, I wanted to go further and make subtle jabs at my supervisor.

But then his wife spoke up and shared her experience as a kid. Her family was heavily involved in a volunteer capacity in a very large church. She didn't like to hear about all the drama, the gossip, the negativity that would sometimes come out of her parents' mouths or from the mouths of those in the church who came over to her home. It was a real struggle for her as she, many times, saw one side of people on Sunday morning and a completely different side the other six days of the week. It was then she said, "You don't want to know too much about how things are in the church because it can corrupt your mind to it all." I've never heard the audible voice of God, but that's about as close to hearing God speak to me, apart from reading something from the Bible, that I'd come. I just knew; God was telling me this through her!

Unfortunately, getting too much in the weeds of a church is a sad reality that most church members struggle with. The more they know about the inner workings of the church, the more discouraged they are about the church. Then they give up on the Church because it's not perfect. It no longer gives off the appearance of everything working in unity. As a pastor, I don't think it's our job to hide everything from church members; authenticity and transparency are a must for leaders in the church. But spilling out our frustrations or disagreements with the people we lead is not beneficial for the Church. We need to speak more positively of Christ's bride, the Church, as well as the people who He died and rose again for who are also on staff.

How do we do that when bad things, mean things, cruel things, and unfair things are done to us, especially when it's by one of our co-workers in the Church? The Apostle Peter gives us some good advice. "Above all, keep loving one another earnestly, since love covers a multitude of sins" (1 Peter 4:8). It's love, the same love God showed us by forgiving sinners like you and me, even though we didn't deserve it. It's a love that only comes from the definition of love. It's a love we can't humanly feel, show, or experience on our own. So we ask for it, constantly. We especially ask for it in moments where all we want to do is stand on a platform and shout our grievances against our church co-laborers.

It was at that moment in our friend's house eating dinner that I began this process of consistently asking God to give me His love for my supervisor, that He would give me loving words to speak to others who ask, and that God's love in me would cover the many sins done against me. Over the next few days and weeks, I would ask for that kind of love over and over again. Wash, rinse, repeat. Because what I wanted most was to be identified as a child of God and for my reputation to represent Jesus well—to everyone, including those who wronged me.

That night, Maria and I went home emotionally spent, even though it was a fun night of hanging out, watching our kids play, and eating good food with friends. This whole "live like Jesus and point people to Jesus" thing was really hard, especially in our current circumstances.

We felt discouraged and overwhelmed by how the next few weeks might unfold. We were not confident in how we might handle things. We may have passed the first two nights of interacting with church people with flying colors, but the next day was going to be my first day back in the office. And Good Friday was four days away, which meant Easter was six days out. How would we do this? How would I do this as a pastor who was supposed to be on his *A*-game around the biggest celebration our faith recognizes?

Before going to bed, we read Philippians 2 as we lay down next to each other. Side Note: It was during this season that we started reading a chapter of Scripture every night together before going to bed. There's nothing overtly spiritual about this, and we don't exegete or discuss it, but it has been a blessing and encouragement to us through everything we have endured. We still do it today, and it has helped bring peace into our marriage relationship. It's also helped us to "not let the sun go down on our anger." If you're married, just try it for a week or two and see how it impacts your marriage.

In our reading, verses three and four stuck out to us. We talked for a minute, prayed, and then we both passed out. But soon after, around midnight, I woke up with a need to write these thoughts down:

> *Do nothing from selfish ambition or conceit" (Philippians 2:3a, NIV). We may want to make people take "our side" in all of this, but that is selfish ambition. We have to put the best for the church leadership and for the flock of the church over what would make us "feel good." "In humility consider others more significant than yourselves" (Philippians 2:3b). I have to count my boss as more significant than myself. That's hard, so hard! Lord, give me [the] grace and strength to do that throughout these next two months. Help me especially do that during this week of Easter. "Not looking to your own interests but each of you to the interests of the others." (Philippians 2:4, NIV). It is now our job to not "pollute the well" at church. We are choosing to put others first by withholding many details, but still be[ing] truthful when the time comes. This is where it will be very difficult. How do we share in a way that protects people, keeps everyone unified, and helps them understand we aren't choosing to leave? We don't have answers for this yet, but I pray that all of our conversations would be seasoned with so much grace and love over these next two months.*

The confidence to "live like Jesus and point people to Jesus" was there in my heart and mind. I was motivated more than ever after reflecting on what the Lord had taught us that night. I hope if you're in this circumstance right now, drop to your knees and ask God to give you that same confidence and encouragement to live like His Son through this hardship. Stop reading this book, pick up a Bible, and dive into Philippians 2. Read it, meditate on it, and ask God to specifically reveal to you what He wants out of you in this season of life.

I closed my journal, went back into our bedroom, lay in our bed, and said this prayer: "In eight hours, I will be at work. By Your grace and through Your love, may I live like I have never lived before, pointing people to Jesus in every conversation that will take place today, the rest of this week, and in the next several weeks and months ahead. I am Your child; use me to point others to Your Son."

Resurrection Power

Hard is an understatement of what I experienced the following week. When everyone was excited and pumped about celebrating Easter, I felt the opposite. There was a buzz around the office the entire week, but I felt disconnected. The week started with my supervisor wanting to meet with me to see how I was doing. By that point, I had processed enough that I was at least able to have an eye-to-eye conversation with him. I shared with him a few things:

One, I was hurt and sad. I was disappointed that he did not give me a fair shot or any warning about the firing. Two, though I did not agree with his decision, I would respect him and not bad-mouth his decision—or him, for that matter. Three, I wanted to leave well; I had no desire to cause drama or discord within the staff when it was revealed that I was fired. With all the turnover that had taken place since I had started, I imagined there'd be a lot of negative talk arising from more staff being fired or quitting. I wanted no part of it, and I told him I'd like to agree on the things that would be communicated to people and the timeframe these things would be communicated.

My supervisor verbalized his understanding of my frustration and sadness but was sticking to his decision. He also appreciated my willingness to leave well and not create discord within the staff. But then things shifted in a strange direction. He agreed we should be on the same page about what we communicate, but we could also agree this was a mutual separation. That we both thought it would be best if I went my separate way.

This took me aback! *Was this not a firing?* Did I not just say two seconds ago that I did *not* agree with his decision? This became moment number one of "in humility, consider others more significant than yourself." I responded kindly, saying, "We can agree on what gets communicated, but me being OK and on the same page with this firing will not be communicated. As I said before, I do not agree with your decision."

There was silence—an eternity of quietness in my mind. Finally, a Holy Spirit thought popped into my head. I say "Holy Spirit thought" because this was not something I had ever thought of or probably would have thought of myself.

"Why don't we communicate that the church leadership has decided to move in a different direction with the leadership of the high school ministry?" My supervisor's pen went immediately to paper, writing that line word for word, like he was copying Scripture from the Bible. He shared how that sounded a lot better than saying I was fired. He didn't want that negative connotation influencing what people thought about me.

Sadly, I knew not saying I was fired was not for me. It was an effort to protect himself and the church leadership when this decision was revealed. Our church had read many email "announcements" in the past two years about staff departures. The more people read, the more people could read between the lines and see the motives behind them. It was at this point I realized my supervisor was not looking out for my interests; he was only looking for damage control and to protect the reputation of church leadership. I had seen this happen a few times in the past year. I had lunches or coffees with my former co-workers who had experienced this "different-direction departure." I knew what was happening, and they would write down every word I said from that point forward to use against me if necessary. I often think this part of the firing experience might be the one church staff who have been fired can relate to most.

Anger and rage burned in my heart toward him, and God laid this verse on my mind: "Take My yoke upon you, and learn from me, for I am gentle (meek) and lowly in heart, and you will find rest for your souls" (Matthew 11:29). I could not bear to have any more conversations with my supervisor if I did not speak in a gentle, meek, and humble manner. If I did not purposefully choose to be meek, I knew anger would grow in my heart, which would turn to rage, which would turn to yelling and losing my temper. So even with my "interests" being pushed aside, I chose to respond gently, no matter what was said, fair or unfair.

Later on, I was reminded of a Messianic prophecy, something written about Jesus hundreds of years before He was born as a baby in a manger: "He will not shout or cry out, or raise his voice in the streets" (Isaiah 42:2). Jesus did not speak up, defend Himself, or protest in front of everyone the injustices He experienced on trial and throughout His crucifixion. I knew I once again had to have His same attitude and voice. This was a challenge for me, not necessarily because I struggled with losing my temper, but because I was naturally a loud person.

I'm one of *those* youth pastors, one who thrives in environments where I get in front of tons of kids or students and capture their attention with just my voice. I even learned how to be really loud in those situations without losing my voice. At camps and retreats, I would be one of the few adults who had a voice left at the end of the week, even though I was the loudest by far. To go from being naturally loud to making a conscious decision to be gentle in my tone was difficult. Yet, as Jesus went through his trial and eventual death, He remained calm. For someone who would've had to project his voice as He taught outdoors to the masses, Jesus didn't raise His voice when false accusations were hurled at Him. He didn't yell at Pilate when he asked Him questions. He didn't even respond to the soldiers who mocked Him; instead, He responded gently, "Father, forgive them for they know not what they do" (Luke 23:34). If I were to be more like Jesus, I realized I would need to make this my intentional attitude and tone as I conversed with my supervisor.

Can the same be said of you? Can you show this type of attitude and tone toward your supervisor who has fired you? Can you daily choose meekness and gentleness over lashing out? For me, anytime I conversed with my supervisor, I repeated Isaiah 42:2 to myself before I started any conversation with him. Wash, rinse, and repeat. Even in the middle of some heated discussions that would take place, the Holy Spirit reminded me of this verse. As you enter a difficult process like this, decide to be like Jesus and choose meekness and gentleness for your tone. Be identified by His love working through you, and gain a reputation of humility and meekness as you interact with others.

A Note to Leaders

Leaders in the church, supervisors who are reading this, I'd like to encourage you to do one thing. Be honest and stand by your decision. Don't try to cover it up; don't try to sugarcoat it. Just be honest when the time comes for any firing to be shared. People will appreciate your honesty and will run away from the foul stench of any "cover-up." Ask yourself this question: If you feel the need to cover up your decision, is it really the right decision? If you feel the need to skew the truth to make it more accepting to the church, then should you be deciding in the first place? If you can still say yes, then attempt to speak transparently and not hide the truth. We will go into more details later about how much to share about a firing, but if it's not the truth, you have no business saying it to people in your church.

Unfortunately, I saw the negative effect this had on our church, specifically our students. When official word came out and then follow-up conversations took place with the church leadership and high school students, it left them more confused, sad, angry, and bitter. So just be honest. If you're confident this is best for your church, don't shy away from it. I don't believe firing someone is a sin, but it can be handled in sinful ways. The more confusion you bring to the situation, the easier it will be to lie, slander, and gossip, and that absolutely breaks the heart of Jesus, the one you have given your life to follow and proclaim. Don't do that to Him; don't hurt His reputation by protecting yours. Don't alienate yourself from God by putting your stamp of approval on your own sin. Don't justify tweaking the truth to protect yourself or "protect" the person you are firing. You will do more harm to yourself if you do that. Through this tough process, honesty will be the only thing that will bring unity and love to what will most likely be a difficult and possibly divisive situation.

4
RESURRECT THE FIRE(D)

My supervisor and I left that conversation agreeing on a couple of lines to use when we shared the news with those on staff, the other ministry leaders, and the students. Nothing would happen that week because of Easter, but we would tell a few key people the following week. General churchgoers and students wouldn't find out for a few more weeks, toward the end of April. I knew this would be hard for me, to be silent for the rest of the holiday week, but I knew it was what was best for the church. On Good Friday and Easter Sunday, I would be the welcoming, extroverted pastor everyone always expected of me. On the inside, however, I was grieving.

He over *me*. I point people to Jesus.

Good Friday morning came, and my supervisor told me I could talk with our counseling pastor about it. He shared how this pastor was let go from a position at a different church about ten years ago. He said I could learn from him by how he processed his experience. Assuming my supervisor had already told this pastor what happened to me, I went into his office a few minutes later and just sat down. And after a few awkward moments of us staring at one another, I spoke up and said, "[My supervisor] didn't tell you, did he?"

It was then I was given my first opportunity to share the news of my firing with a member of our church family. I was scared about "losing it" or slandering my supervisor, but I could communicate the couple of things that we had agreed were appropriate to share. "My philosophy of ministry is different from the church's. The leadership wants to move in a new direction with the high school ministry. . . . I was affirmed as a 'good' youth pastor but not as a good fit for this church."

As I spoke, I watched the telltale signs of disbelief come over the pastor's face: He raised his eyebrows, widened his eyes, and his jaw slowly opened. He prodded me for more information, namely the "real" reasons I was fired, but I told him that was all I was going to say. If he wanted to learn more, he could ask my supervisor. And so he did!

He literally stood up and headed to the office next to his, which was my supervisor's office. I sat where I was for a few minutes, listening to the rumblings and murmurs of what I determined was a heated discussion. Then the counseling pastor came back into his office and said, "The three of us will meet first thing next week when everyone is back in the office. I have no clue what he is thinking, but we are not done here."

Shock exploded inside me. I didn't know what to say (this will happen a lot in my story). Was he trying to get me my job back? Was he going to mediate the situation to help us work together? Thankfully, the pastor had a scheduled counseling appointment at that moment with someone from our church, so the conversation had to end there. I left his office, unsure about what was next but thankful I didn't have to go into details with anyone else just yet.

I maneuvered through Good Friday and Easter Sunday. I kept my focus on the salvation I did not deserve from Jesus and on this new opportunity to become more like Jesus. I still did not know what to expect from the upcoming meeting. So I wrote this in my journal the morning before we met:

> *Lord, I really don't know what is going to come from this conversation. I know you can work miracles and can turn hard hearts into soft hearts; I just don't know if this is the time. I feel as if you have called me to a greater purpose—to use this unfair experience to bless and encourage many pastors who will have to be on either side of a firing. And like I wrote before, I don't want to see the church implode because of my firing. But Lord, I ask that you make it happen quickly. Lord, if he truly does repent, would you give me the grace and humility I need to work for him again?*

Later on Easter Sunday night, the counseling pastor (CP) called me. He shared with me all the conversations he had over the course of the weekend. I discovered zero elders knew I was being fired. Zero! The elders were informed that a staff person was being let go at the end of the ministry year, but not who because, in this church, elders do not have any input or oversight with staffing decisions. My supervisor informed the senior pastor what he was planning to do and then pulled in the other campus pastor who sat in on the firing conversation. That was it. The CP also talked with two of the people from the now infamous church consulting group, and they were just as baffled and confused as the elders were about this decision.

The consulting group had laid out a specific six-step process that we, as leaders, were supposed to go through with staff and volunteers who were not "doing well" in their ministries. Letting someone go because we thought they were not a good fit was not an option; we needed to work with each individual and find out how they could serve either in our ministry or a different ministry within the church. This six-step process would take time, energy, and effort . . . and a clear expectation was supposed to be set for the volunteers/leaders that they were entering an "improvement plan" process. From the consultants' perspective, my supervisor did none of those things, but the opposite of what they taught.

While the CP was on the phone with me, he informed me the consulting group was now calling my supervisor to talk through all of this. Again, I felt taken aback. I didn't know what to say. The CP told me to be prepared to honestly share my perspective about the whole situation the next day, and we would go from there. I hung up the phone and asked God to give me humility, peace, and grace as the conversation drew near.

Let's Get Ready to Rumble

In Tuesday's conversation—and in the many others I didn't know I was going to have—I really wanted to work hard at not disrespecting my supervisor in person. Even more, I had to pursue respect behind his back, when he was not in the room or when I would have to share this news with someone else. I chose to carefully watch my tone, posture, other non-verbals, and, obviously, the words I would use.

The CP started the conversation by letting us both know of the different conversations he had engaged in over the past five days. After that, the CP wanted to hear from my supervisor the reason he made this decision to fire me.

As my supervisor outlined the list of reasons, I prayed God would allow me to speak wisely and kindly in any of my responses. But I didn't get a chance to talk; instead, the CP questioned the reasons, pushing back on my supervisor's thought process. For the next thirty minutes, they went back and forth, the CP fighting almost as if he was the one being fired. I could see this was going nowhere, and I believe the CP did as well.

Finally, he asked me a question. "Could you have done anything differently over these last few months that would have avoided getting to this place?" Well, I had all the answers since I had gone rogue and copied my supervisor's notes the week before. I shared this statement as I looked directly at my supervisor: "I could've worked harder and shown more effort to work with you. I don't think you saw me as a team player, and that is something I need to change wherever God has me next." The CP then asked my supervisor the same question, and his response was quite different. There was a long pause, some uttering of "uhs" and "wells," before he said, "I would really have to process that more, but right now, I don't think so." And that was it. He was just as confident of his rightness the day he fired me as he was that day.

I left that meeting feeling dejected and hurt. I wrote in my journal later that night.

> *God, give me the grace to show to my boss. It was sad to hear him say he had 'to process' ways he could've done things differently and better. It hurt not to see an ounce of forgiveness and repentance, but an even greater confidence that he was right in his decision, conduct, and management of me. There was a small hope in me [of getting] my job back. So, it definitely stung to not even get anything out of him. God, you must have different ideas in mind for me, so help me trust you and not be frustrated with being ripped away from this ministry.*
>
> *Even though I shared a specific of what I learned and what I could've done better, I don't think I could've made his top priorities for the ministry my top priorities. I don't know, maybe I could have, but hindsight is 20/20. It may have worked for a bit, but I think we most likely would have gotten to this same place. I still feel like he gave up on me. Lord, you really confirmed that today, and that hurts. I wouldn't have been mentored or trained in a way that I would have profited spiritually*

> *from. God, if I continue in church ministry, I pray I can find pastor(s) and staff who will mentor me.*

I was filled with God's grace and knew that even though I was hurt, I needed to move forward because the next couple of days were when this information would be shared with a few staff people and close friends within the church. The one thing I took away from these initial conversations was this: Everyone will take this news a different way. In the same way, people will care for you in whatever way is most comfortable for them, they will also react in ways they normally react to shocking and difficult news. People will care for you in whatever way is most comfortable for them, they will also react in ways they normally react to shocking and difficult news.

People will care for you in whatever way is most comfortable for them, they will also react in ways they normally react to shocking and difficult news.

The Initial Revelations

I'm thankful the Lord allowed me to see three drastically different reactions (four if you count the CP) in the first week of my firing. It reminded me of how the disciples reacted differently to Jesus telling them He was going to be betrayed and eventually die. Peter rebuked Jesus. Judas felt guilty and ran off. John tried to have a private conversation with Jesus to figure out who it was who'd betray him. Even before that, the Sons of Thunder were jockeying for position to be the greatest when Jesus told them they couldn't handle what He was going to endure.

The first staff person to find out was the other youth pastor I worked closely with, and to say he was shocked would be an understatement. My supervisor was there to share the news while I sat silently. My supervisor gave me a couple of minutes to talk with him before he took him to lunch and offered him leadership responsibility over the sixth to twelfth-grade ministries, with the potential of receiving some administrative help in the next month or two. The irony of this offer was that my co-laborer in youth ministry did not like working for my supervisor. I had spent much of the past year offering feedback about how to get along with him and see things from each other's perspective. I later learned in their lunch conversation, the other youth pastor expressed his anger toward our supervisor about my firing, told him "no" to the job offer, and defended me more than anything else.

After lunch, he came back to my office and vented to me for almost an hour. He was mad; he felt like he was being manipulated with this "opportunity" to lead when what he believed was that it was all about damage control. If one consistent face was present for the high school students, then the storm could be weathered, especially with so many graduating eighth graders staying with their beloved junior high pastor into the high school transition.

I felt he was more focused on himself than on me, but I realized in that conversation, I was there to care for him. I had already endured two weeks to process all of this; he had just found out and was now going to be the one who was supposed to keep everything moving forward. That would be an overwhelming task. I needed to let him vent, tell him I was sorry he had been thrust into this awkward, lose-lose situation. I knew how he operated: when unknowns or frustrations came his way, he needed the space to outwardly process things, saying what was on his heart, and then, he was good. By the end of his venting, he began to care for me, asking me how I was doing, praying for me, and being a good brother and friend.

Two other staff members found out later that week, and they had two different reactions. The children's director I worked with didn't question the decision in front of my supervisor. She didn't want to know the details of it; instead, she gave me compliment after compliment while the three of us sat in the meeting. "I know this will be handled professionally by Kyle. He is not the type of person to spread rumors or create drama. He has not done that in the past year with all the other transitions, and I know he will shine the light of Christ to all during this time . . . I am sure he will carefully and kindly articulate this information to the students and families and still show them the love of Jesus . . . I know anything negative that might be said or spread in those next couple of weeks won't come from him. Kyle will handle this with the utmost integrity as he always has in the two years I've worked with him."

Honestly, I didn't give a rip about my integrity or character. Deep down, I wanted her to ask the tough questions and make my supervisor squirm. I wanted her to see the side of him I had been dealing with over the past two weeks. That mindset and hope were selfish on my part, and I never verbalized these things to her because she was the type of person who did not like conflict. If she could remove herself from the conflict and believe the best about someone, she would. Even in our private conversation after the fact, she reiterated she knew I would leave well and did not want to know any of the details.

The other staff person was married, and my wife and I were mentoring her and her husband. Her husband wasn't able to come over the night we had invited them for dinner because he got sick, but we still had her over and shared the news. As I explained everything to her, she acted like we were having a normal conversation, like it was just a typical meeting at work about an event or project or something . . . neutral. She gave little reaction to it, said she was sorry maybe once or twice, and was more concerned about how the students would react when they heard this news. Why? Well, she had been serving in the church's student ministry for the past five years. She had seen the devastation the high turnover rate had inflicted on the student ministry and, more specifically, the students' faith. It was almost as if she had become numb to it herself—and maybe she was. She had seen it all too often. This was the third firing in this ministry in the last five years, and this would be another mentoring relationship that would abruptly end for reasons outside of her control. Sometimes numbness can outweigh frustration.

Previous Revelations

Reality was setting in, and it gave me some more time for God to speak to me before the upcoming Wednesday when our entire staff would find out the news and later that weekend when the students and parents would also find out.

I thought of the parents I'd had in my ministry over the years, specifically about the times I had to tell them their students had a "bad night" at youth group. Some defended their kids immediately and blamed other students in the youth group; others came down on their students harshly, right in front of me. Some sat there quietly before responding with, "We will talk more about this with him or her when we get home." It's a natural, human response to handle unpleasant information differently. That's what helped me mentally and emotionally prepare for the conversations I was about to have with people over the next few weeks. I knew I couldn't expect everyone to go to battle for me and boycott the church (in fact, none of them would do that, and that wouldn't have been good, either). Some would experience sadness, others anger, while some would feel shock and still others wouldn't know what to say.

Can we expect anything else? I don't think so because if Jesus didn't expect a standard response from His disciples, why should we expect one from our community? Be content with how people respond to your firing, and know that no one will care for you perfectly. No one will respond exactly how you want them to, but all of them need to go through the same process of dealing with this news as you. This is what makes leading God's people—or, in biblical terms, *shepherding* God's sheep—a challenge and a joy . . . caring for each sheep the way the Good Shepherd has wired them to be cared for. As a pastor, when you find that opportunity to truly care for someone after many failed attempts to crack their outer shell, it's a day of celebration! When they are in their most vulnerable state, hearing this sad news from you, allow them to react differently and be OK with whatever that looks like. And even if you're not in a pastoral position, be content with people who respond differently; don't put the unrealistic expectation on them to care for you perfectly because they won't. They can't.

Feel the Burn

As I had my conversations, I knew I had to keep going, dig deeper, and allow God to refine me more and more. This is so hard (so, so hard): to continue putting yourself back into the fire(d). To read God's Word with a mindset that allows Him to convict your heart to change when, in all honesty, you feel like it's your supervisor that could use a little bit more Bible in their life! You have to be intentional to grow from your firing, not getting complacent with what you have already learned and experienced. It's counter-intuitive to pick the scab off of your emotional wound, but there is powerful work God wants to do inside you, and it gets done every time you decide to lean into your pain and obey Him.

I've included some Bible verses that God brought to light as I kept going back to the fire(d). God impressed upon my heart to read through the book of Ephesians. Chapter 4 (NIV) had many convicting verses, which helped me pursue this refining:

- vs. 2–3: I need to walk with all humility, gentleness, and patience, bearing with everyone in love, to be eager to maintain the unity of the Spirit in the bond of peace. Am I eager to keep peace and unity with my church as I leave?
- v. 15: When I speak the truth in love, I mature in Christ. Am I going to see that in every conversation I have moving forward, I can mature in Christ by how I speak?

- vs. 25–27: When I speak with my supervisor, my brother in Christ, I cannot let my anger lead me toward sinning against him. How do I prevent the devil from taking advantage of my anger?
- vs. 29–32: In every conversation and interaction I have moving forward, I need to pursue these four things: Build everyone up (29), don't grieve the Holy Spirit (30), put away bitterness and slander (31), and forgive as Christ forgave me (32). If I can remember these four things consistently, they will help me leave well without damaging the Bride.

Ephesians 6 (NIV) also jumped out to me.

- vs. 5–8: I have to serve my boss as I would serve Jesus; and to be honest, I have zero desire to do that—zero. I need to work with enthusiasm because it is the Lord I am ultimately working for, not anyone else. This is what *has* to motivate me over these next few weeks as I finish. (As I wrote these thoughts in my journal, I battled the desire to even go to youth group that night; I wanted to just break off those relationships and be done with them to avoid more pain and hurt). But if I am serving Jesus alone, then I have to finish well!
- v. 12: The battle is not against my supervisor or my church; it is against Satan. It's against the evil powers of this world! Even though I may feel like my supervisor is the enemy, I must align my feelings and heart with

God's. This means allowing this truth to roll around in my mind and heart when I think he's the enemy. The tendency is for our hearts and feelings to contradict what God's Word says. That's why we have to willingly and intentionally align our hearts to what His Word says. I knew as the information of my firing would be shared publicly over the coming weeks, it would be so easy to paint my supervisor as the enemy because I felt he had wronged me and hurt me so much. And Satan would love for me to do that; he wants to steal the joy I find in Jesus. Sharing with truth *and* grace would be the only way Satan couldn't gain a foothold on my anger (My prayer in my journal was for God to give me continuous wisdom about what I should share and what I should withhold).

- v. 18: I have to "stay alert" because sin is already creeping back into my heart. I could feel myself giving in to lust. I had three arguments with my wife over three days, right before this information went public. I noticed how selfish I was being. Staying alert for me was the desire to persistently pray in the Spirit against my sinful tendencies and desires, specifically when my frustration leads me to sin. I once heard in a sermon, "Don't let your discouragement lead to disobedience." Yup, that was me.

The last bit of Scripture that spoke to Maria and me during this fateful week was 1 Peter 4:8 (NIV). Here is a paragraph from my journal entry about this verse:

How do I continue to show grace to my boss when he exaggerates some of his issues with me as well as when he says completely untrue things about who I am, what I do, or what the ministry is doing? Love toward him will cover a multitude of sins that are done against me! I need you, Spirit, to give me a desire to forgive, to let go of bitterness, to be freed from the bondage of wanting to be right and get[ting] back at him. I don't need to let this eat at me because God, you will judge our hearts and motives and words; you will right all wrongs in your own time and [in] your own way. Help me be a humble conduit of your grace and love.

Moving through the Fire(d)

In the weeks following my initial conversations, I entered a crossroads about what I should do next for a career. Knowing my wife was physically incapable of working, I would need to find a job by July 1—when severance and, more importantly, insurance would be over. When my youth pastor who had been fired in the past talked to me the day after I was fired, he asked me if I wanted to continue in ministry. He had taken a break for over a year from full-time ministry before heading back into pastoral ministry. For me, though I was emotionally defeated, I still had a strong desire to work with students . . . and work within the Church. So he told me to look for jobs right away. It was spring, which is the time of year when churches are in transition with some of their staff. This was a good time to be looking, so I jumped on the normal websites with open church positions.

It was not necessarily a new process for me since I had used these websites for my first two youth ministry jobs, but it was weird to not be searching on my timeframe as I had in the past. I was being forced to search, and it made me feel I'd lost control of my life. I hated that feeling. Yet, control was exactly what God wanted in my life. It's not like He didn't have control because He's God, but I was not in a place of total submission to Him when it came to "my" career. Yes, I chose to go into full-time ministry as a junior in high school and forgo many scholarship opportunities for college athletics to go to a Bible college to prepare for ministry. But now, at this point in my life, I had tried to take control so I could "move up the ladder" or "make it bigger" in the ministry world. God would not allow that anymore.

Here's the crazy thing: the first job opening I saw was at a church less than thirty minutes from our home. I immediately applied and the next week, was having lunch with the campus pastor. It was a smaller campus of a larger multi-site church where the campus pastor and the youth pastor were the only two full-time positions, with a couple of part-time staff. In our conversation, I found out that only four months before coming into this position, the campus pastor was forced to resign from his position at his previous church. He was there for barely a year after being a lead pastor of a church for ten-plus years. He was going from a thousand-plus-member church to the "200 on Easter Sunday" campus. He said starting there felt like "a step backward," and when I applied for this new position, I felt the same thing.

Yet the Lord was clearly refining my prideful heart and revealing to me that He was in control of where He puts His leaders, and He doesn't care about the number of people who show up every weekend. He will put me exactly where I need to be, and He will put you exactly where you need to be in this world to do His Kingdom work. I needed to hear that from this pastor, and, really, from God too. I didn't need to be picky about what job I was going to do next; I just needed to seek the Spirit's leading for which door He wanted me to walk through. Learning this lesson in the first week of searching for a new job was significant for what I would choose next in my career.

I don't necessarily have advice for those of you who are now deciding if you want to go back into full-time ministry or work in the business world. I have seen pastors jump right into ministry immediately and others take years off, some never getting back into full-time ministry. The decision may be easy for you if only one opportunity presents itself and the bills need to be paid soon. But if you have options, really seek the Lord in it. Don't just view opportunities from a natural, human perspective (e.g., the location, the type of ministry/job, the pay, the benefits). But get on your hands and knees daily and ask God to guide your next steps.

There may be a huge faith risk moving forward (most likely there will be), but there will be peace in whatever decision you make because you have sought the Lord in it. I know when I took my second youth pastor job at the church I was now being fired from, my wife never had that peace. And if I'm honest, I never did, either. It made sense on paper—a lot of sense on paper. But there was not enough seeking the Lord in it; there was not enough prayer devoted to this decision. We knew we were called to leave our first church, and I trusted God had placed us here at the second church for purposes greater than we could ever have imagined, but the decision lay too much on us (more specifically, on me) and less on God.

A Note to Leaders

One thing I've noticed over the past few years as a senior leader is I can easily fall prey to the idea that if someone doesn't agree with me, has a different idea than me, or has constructive feedback for me, they must be against the church and not for the church. I'm embarrassed to admit it, but I have too often resonated with King Saul when he was chasing David around, trying to kill him, and protecting his kingdom lineage. We saw how that ended for King Saul, but it is very easy to slide into this unhealthy pattern of putting our vision, ideas, and plans on the pedestal of "special revelation from God."

So, to combat those feelings, what if we started with the assumption that our staff and leaders are actually for the church, for us, and for the Gospel?

If we believe the best in them, that their hearts are truly being led by the Holy Spirit and they have a strong desire for people to know and love Jesus, then, when they are struggling—not performing, not aligning—we choose to help and encourage instead of criticize and move on. Instead of thinking there must be something wrong with them, we dig a little deeper to figure out why things may be wrong *in them*.

In doing so, we may also see the things that are wrong *in us;* that God needs to change *within our hearts*. Our care and compassion will show them we are for them and in turn, it will remind us that they are for us, for the church, and for the mission of advancing the Gospel.

Leaders, view and treat them as people who are your equals: created in the image of God, loved and valued enough that Jesus died in their places (and yours), and who rose again so that we can be restored to a right relationship with God—forever!

5
NO NEED FOR JASON

The weekend was over. Tuesday was the day my supervisor, the counseling pastor (CP), and I were finalizing the wording of the email. The next day, we would initiate the communication plan for the staff.

Just before the meeting began, the CP asked me if he could have a couple of minutes alone with my supervisor before I entered. I obliged, and an hour later, I was finally pulled into the office. I didn't know what they had talked about for that long.

My supervisor kicked off the conversation by saying that after talking with the CP for the last hour and really listening to the Lord over the weekend, he sensed a "renewed desire in me" to earn my job back, a "willingness to work with him." That certainly wasn't what I was expecting!

The two of them had also discussed how they would both be willing to enter into a few weeks of conversations to see if my firing was the right decision. We would press pause on our communication plan, tell the few people who already knew that this decision was not finalized, and dig deeper into our differences to understand whether the firing was best for everyone. They also said they would not force me into this conversation. If I didn't want to stay on board, I could push forward with the communication plan like we had agreed on last week.

I didn't know what to say. I said the only thought that popped into my head: "I have to talk with my wife" (anytime you think you need to talk with your spouse, that is always the correct response, so listen and act upon it). I asked them if I could have twenty-four hours to process this new strategy with Maria, and they agreed. We ended the meeting and put it on our calendars to meet first thing the next morning.

I immediately left the office; I could barely hold in the tears as I left the church and walked to my car. On my drive home, I completely broke down, screaming at God, "WHAT ARE YOU DOING?!?!?!" over and over and over again. It lasted almost fifteen minutes—no exaggeration. I somewhat composed myself as I entered my home, but my wife could tell I had been crying—OK, bawling my eyes out. We spoke more about this turn of events throughout the rest of the day and even more so after the kids went to bed. We spent time praying with one another and this is what we felt the Lord was calling us to do, which I wrote in my journal:

> *God, I have no idea what you are doing! The only clear thought I have is that you are making us more like Jesus, drawing out all aspects of humility, grace,*

and forgiveness, which I need to emulate from Christ's life. Thank you for using my wife to speak this truth into my life. She really is so wise in discerning what you are calling us to do. I pray that even in my most negative and frustrating moments, you would give her grace and patience with me and an even greater discerning spirit when it comes to what we have to do over these next few weeks.

Lord, I'm not sensing my boss has any humility or a desire to seek forgiveness or even admit any wrongdoing in all of this. It's so hard to be in this situation and lean into the trial. Oh, God, give me the strength, the courage, the perseverance. Create in me a desire to be humble and quick to listen, even if my boss is not. You are really stretching me in all of this, but I see you continuing to break down my pride and my need for control. I don't know what you have in store for us; I don't know how you are working in all of this, but I pray you would make yourself clear where you want us to go in these next couple of months.

In this process of conversations, I still need to be pursuing other ministry options. If we continue to see the dysfunction and a lack of willingness to change, we strongly believe that you are calling us out of this church. As well, we are boldly asking for significant conversations or even an offer from another church if you are calling us out and sending us to a new place.

You know the care that my wife needs right now and having something in place by July 1st is important to her healing.

Lord, here are three things we sense you are doing and want me to share tomorrow. 1) I need to reiterate that I am still fired so that my severance package (and, most importantly, the insurance for Maria) does not change. 2) I need to see some sort of forgiveness in my boss's heart tomorrow, acknowledging that he has indeed caused hurt and pain [within] me. 3) As I pursue clarity, I need my boss to give me much clarity about his expectations moving forward.

The next morning, I shared those three things with my supervisor and the CP, and they both agreed those were fair terms to work within. With everyone in agreement, we moved forward with these conversations. The CP agreed to moderate the discussions between us and not give too much input into anything we talk about. As well, he suggested that our first conversation would be focused on where the two of us "got off track." We would both look back over the past six months to learn where we did not always see eye-to-eye and "work backward to move forward." Both of us agreed this was a good starting point, and we would define the parameters of future conversations after this initial conversation.

I ended the conversation by asking my supervisor if he could see how he had hurt me over the past few weeks, and he acknowledged he "could *possibly* have done things differently."

It wasn't much, but it was a start, and I had only asked the Lord to show me "some sort" of forgiveness in his heart. That was "some sort" in my book.

Round One: Déjà Vu

I entered this first conversation with cautious optimism, hoping clarity would be achieved above everything else. I had worked hard at preparing detailed notes of different conversations my supervisor and I had in the past six months, times when I knew there was tension and disagreement. The morning leading up to the meeting, I could sense the Holy Spirit prompting me to let my supervisor start the conversation—to hear from him first, to not get defensive, to seek humility in posture and tone, to seek understanding about his perspective, and to not focus on being understood. Once again, as I entered this first conversation, I had no idea this was what the Lord had for me.

After the CP prayed, he asked how we wanted to start the conversation. I responded that I wanted to hear from my supervisor first. I wanted him to share, from his perspective, the ways he and I had veered off track over the last six months. We all agreed, and my supervisor began talking . . . but not about that. Instead, he handed the CP and me a five-page, single-spaced document entitled, "Growth Areas in Order to Maintain Employment (with a Probationary Period)."

My supervisor shared that over the last two days, he thought about what the student ministry needed to be at our church and how I should fit into the vision as the leader going forward. He then spent the next hour and a half going through his document. It was broken into four sections of "improvement," and there were thirty bullet points between the four sections. Each bullet point had a specific growth area and a description of what success would look like in the student ministry.

As was becoming a frequent occurrence, I didn't know what to say. It didn't matter, though, because I never got a chance to say anything. He never paused for feedback or questions; he just kept talking, telling me what I had to do to stay employed. There was no conversation, only what felt like condemnation. He was right; I was wrong, and this was how it was going to be.

Halfway through this time, I mustered up the courage to interrupt and asked if we could press pause on covering the last two sections of the document so I could share some thoughts. This was not what he had in mind; he wanted to cover everything first. Once again, I felt the Holy Spirit giving me that same nudge to relinquish having to be heard or understood, but to hear and understand. These verses came to mind: "And the chief priests accused him of many things. And Pilate again asked him, 'Have you no answer to make? See how many charges they bring against you.' But Jesus made no further answer, so that Pilate was amazed" (Mark 13:3–5). So I paused, said OK, and he continued going through his document.

The CP could tell I was beaten up after the word assault, so he ended the meeting by saying, "Let's pray and next week, we'll pick this back up. Kyle, you can start the conversation by responding to some of these growth areas shared." I closed my eyes with a mixed bag of emotions tumbling around within me: anger, sadness, frustration, hopelessness, and discouragement. We prayed, then I looked up, said thanks to my supervisor, and left.

It was like déjà vu, that same feeling I had three weeks ago after being fired—that's how I felt after this "conversation." It was like being fired again, a second firing from the same job and the same supervisor. Only this time, I didn't need to go into Jason Bourne mode to figure out why I was being fired. I had been bombarded with every specific reason known to humankind. It was strange, surreal, and overwhelming, except this time, I wasn't crying or holding back tears. I felt groggy. It was like first waking up in the morning and not having all your bearings yet—that's how I felt as I walked back to my office. I sat at my desk and stared blankly at my computer.

The CP came into my office a minute later and asked me what I thought. I took a breath and explained that I felt fired again, but that was it. I couldn't wrap my mind around the thirty bullet points of improvement or even recite the notes I took on the paper, as my supervisor described each point. I'm not sure if I was in actual "shock," but I imagine it was close. The CP shared his thoughts, and we were on the same page. What happened wasn't what he expected this "conversation" to be (or what we had all decided); it was not a conversation at all, and he could see how it felt like a second firing. He asked me if he could look over my notes, and I let him. After a few minutes of silence, he said, "The one phrase you wrote down the most on these five sheets of paper is 'I'm already doing this!'"

Ignorance Is Bliss, Maybe

The CP and I spoke more about this phrase as I came out of my foggy state, and the core issue we observed was twofold.

1) My supervisor was not aware of what was actually happening in the high school ministry. The things he expected me to do, which he thought would be changes, were already happening under my leadership. Whether it was programming, leadership development, professional skills, or something else. I wrote this phrase by two-thirds of the points, twenty out of thirty! Which led to the next thought conclusion:

2) The CP pointed out that I most likely had not communicated all these things to my supervisor if I was already doing them. And once again, this was a both/and issue (both my supervisor and I had ownership of this). I realized then that I had the impression my supervisor was too busy to want to know the minor details of what I was doing in the ministry because he was overseeing so much at our church. Even though he never asked me about these specific things, I didn't share them with him from the beginning. And for leaders, this is the point we need to remember: the employer/employee relationship is a two-way street. Investment needs to happen on both sides, just like with any relationship. The best relationships require both individuals to pursue communication consistently.

The employer/employee relationship is a two-way street. Investment needs to happen on both sides, just like with any relationship. The best relationships require both individuals to pursue communication consistently.

Neither of us did a good job at pursuing; both of us had the expectation the other would be the driving communicating force in this relationship. Even if I felt bombarded and overwhelmed by this first "conversation," I had to own it. He was ignorant of what was happening, and I was ignorant of his desire to know what was happening. It was anything but blissful.

So what does this look like in your leaders/staff relationship? If you're the employer—the supervisor—have you intentionally pursued knowing not only the details of your staff's ministry but care about how and why they do it? Have you laid out clear guidelines about when you want certain things communicated? Are these communication pieces done verbally in one-on-one meetings, in front of other staff, or electronically and submitted to you alone, to elders, to other senior leaders? As a supervisor, you must set the parameters of what clear, consistent communication looks like with your staff members. More importantly, you have to set an example of what you expect from them: you inspect what you expect.

If you're a staff member, put yourself in the shoes of your leader. What things would you want to know? What would you expect from a person who was in your position in ministry? Write those down and look to communicate those things consistently. If you are over-communicating or sharing too much with your supervisor, they will let you know. If you take the initiative when they are not, it will force them to respond with clarity about what they want from you.

Round Two: Make Disciples

During the following weekend, I came out of the fog, realizing this truth about communication and beginning to formulate some thoughts to bring back to our "second conversation."

I started our meeting with honesty, explaining how I felt he had missed the point of the first meeting, that it ended up not feeling like a conversation but a "second firing." I also shared with him that many of the bullet points he had listed for growth areas I had already been doing. I owned up to the fact that I did not clearly communicate those things to him throughout my last nine months working for him, but I would do a better job with that now that I knew he wanted to see and know these things about the ministry.

I chose not to focus on defending myself because there were a few more bullet points I needed even more clarity on from him to get down to the heart of what he truly wanted from me. I did not feel like I was doing these four bullet points and, in fact, would have issues being forced to do them if I were to continue working at the church. I could tell he was not happy with my opinion of it not being a conversation, so I asked him what he thought before I asked clarifying questions about those four bullet points.

He didn't say anything at first, then he asked the CP what he thought the purpose of these conversations was and how he thought Friday's conversation went. The CP kindly affirmed my take on Friday's "conversation." He did not discount the information my supervisor had to share, but he, too, felt it had gone off course from where we had all agreed to go. My supervisor was visibly angry and said, "What's the purpose of these meetings? Aren't they to see if Kyle can still work here? Am I missing something?" I could tell things might escalate quickly, so I stepped in and said, "I agree these conversations are about my future employment, but last week did not feel like a conversation. I took seriously everything you said and made tons of notes about it." I showed him my paper and continued, "But we didn't converse; you talked, and we listened. I just want today to be about both of us—maybe even the three of us—talking. That's all." Though he still seemed frustrated, he agreed to move forward.

There were two bullet points that dealt directly with my time. He had written, but not clearly explained, that I spent too much time focused on my family on Sunday mornings, and I must start working the normal 8:30 a.m. to 5:00 p.m. office schedule instead of my modified schedule of 7:30 a.m. to 4:00 p.m. So I asked what his purpose was for the two bullet points.

First, he perceived I focused too much on my kids and wife on Sunday mornings. The main purpose for me on a Sunday morning was to engage and connect with any families and students in the church. I asked him to clarify how I was not doing this up to his standards, and he said, "I just see you spending too much time with your family, and it distracts you from engaging with other people on a Sunday morning."

My wife had not been to church for over two months because of her injury. My kids were not coming with me, and it was my volunteer leaders who would get to my house at 8:00 a.m. and spend the morning with them to help while I was at church until 1:00 p.m. So I shared that when my family *was there*, I needed to help my wife get both kids out of the van, get them checked into their classrooms, then between services, when almost everyone had left and no one had yet arrived for the second service, I would help get my kids back into their car seats, into the van, and send them on their way. I estimated that all of this took about fifteen minutes. I further clarified, "I spend fifteen minutes out of five hours on a Sunday morning focused on my family. Is that too much?"

Yes, yes, it was. I was taken aback; I didn't know what to say as my heart sank and my stomach felt sick. The CP, who is usually next to me in the church lobby most Sundays, chimed in with his opinion. "I see him with his family and within those 'fifteen minutes,' there are flocks of students and parents around him. His family, more so his wife and kids, are a magnet for people. That 'fifteen minutes' might be his best engagement of people every Sunday."

My boss simply responded, "I just don't see it. I disagree." When we pressed him to give examples, he kept repeating, "I just don't see it."

Frustrated, I moved on to the second point of working an 8:30–5:00 schedule instead of the 7:30–4:00 schedule I had worked since I started almost two years before.

He clarified, "You miss opportunities to engage with senior leadership or the senior pastor when you leave right at 4:00 p.m. This is not a culture where we leave right at 5:00 p.m. but are always willing to stay a little later to make sure the job gets done." What I learned from my supervisor was that our senior pastor was only in the office in the late afternoons for meetings, and then he used that last hour to drop by other staff offices to chat with them. So it was perceived that because I was gone, I must not be working hard or giving enough effort like everyone else (once again, before COVID-19, give them some slack!). I understood his point but reminded him why I had this schedule and why I needed to maintain this schedule.

My wife and I had scheduled out months of appointments for the chiropractor, physical therapist, and therapeutic massages. I drove fifteen minutes to get home, got my kids ready, and drove everyone thirty minutes to an appointment. While my wife had her hour-long appointment, I would get dinner and play with my kids at a local library, playground, or somewhere similar. Then we picked her up, drove back home through the wonderful Chicago suburbs' rush-hour traffic, and got our kids to bed. Four days a week, three hours a night, that was our life in this season. Staying until 5:00 p.m. instead of 4:00 p.m. would not only start that process later, but our various helpers couldn't stay until 5:00 p.m., leaving my wife alone with kids she physically could not take care of without some assistance. And all of our travel times would take twice as long because of the rush-hour traffic in the Chicagoland area. If I had to make this shift, we would have to reschedule months of appointments with three different doctors' offices, along with trying to configure multiple schedules of people who were with my wife and kids daily.

I had just word-vomited at his feet, and it was as if he saw the vomit by his feet, looked at it, and said, "Clean it up yourself" and walked away. Translation: He reiterated his point that if I wanted to maintain employment at the church, I would need to make the sacrifice and figure it out. I looked over at the CP and said, "Could you close out this meeting in prayer?" He did, and I left, never making eye contact with my supervisor.

Anger, sadness, and a wide mix of other emotions filled my heart as I left that day, but one thing was clear: I now had a picture of what empathy was *and wasn't*. I went home that night, and on our ride to the doctor's office, I told my wife the conversation that had taken place. She started crying, and I said, "Don't worry. I will not be working there anymore. The

Lord will be faithful to provide a new opportunity for us that will give us the flexibility we need in these wilderness seasons." As I said those words to her, a great peace came over me, and I knew the Lord was indeed removing us from this working environment.

Later that night, I was reminded of a book I read in seminary by Andy Stanley entitled *When Work and Family Collide*. In it, he shares this tension between church planting and needing to be home to help his wife with their three little kids at a certain time every day. He writes, "So, in my own way, I made a deal with God. Essentially, I said, 'Lord, feel free to build whatever kind of church you can build with forty-five hours of my time. You know that's all I have right now.'"[7] I shared that insight with my wife that night before bed, adding, "Hey, if Andy Stanley can start a mega-church working forty-five hours a week and still make sure he leaves work at 4:00 p.m. every day, I think God will give us something like that in this season of our life too."

Leaders . . . supervisors, *this is the church*. This is not a corporate business—though there are business aspects within the Church, where you need to clock in and clock out, where the "success" of your "company" is driven by a hard, bottom line. But the Church is most importantly *Christ's Bride*, so why do we struggle to show compassion toward and offer care for our staff when they are enduring hard times? Why does the job a person performs overshadow the person?

Why does the job a person performs overshadow the person?

7 Stanley, Andy. 2011. *When Work and Family Collide: Keeping Your Job from Cheating Your Family*. Multnomah.

If there is a trait I have noticed is missing from most leaders in the Church, it's empathy toward their staff. How can you expect those who are not being filled up by their leaders to pour into those they are leading and serving within their ministries?

Carey Nieuwhof wrote this in one of his blog posts from September 20, 2018, and it stuck out to me then and stayed with me over the years: "Competency is what gets you in the room, but character is what keeps you in it."[8] In this context, if you are an employer, leader, or senior-level pastor at a church, it probably wasn't your empathy that got you to your place of leadership. But your empathy is what will help your team thrive and grow; it will make people want to work for you, want to sacrifice for the Church, and want to pour out to others because they are being cared for by you. Empathy will remind you that your call to make disciples within the context of a local church starts with your staff, your employees. It is not about hiring staff and leading them to work for the ministry of the church. It's about making disciples of your staff, loving them in the same way Jesus loved and served His disciples. After all, that's how we show God's love. We know He first loved us, and that love gives us the power to love others.

Round Three: Beginning of the End

As I entered the final conversation, I knew I was done working at this church. No matter what was said in this meeting, I knew I could not sacrifice my time with my family in the way that was

8 Nieuwhof, Carey. 2022. "Why The Smartest Leaders Move Way Beyond Their To-Do List To Accomplish Far More." n.d., www.careynieuwhof.com.

being asked of me. So I entered this conversation with a little more boldness than in the past, knowing I could confidently share what I thought leading a high school ministry looked like and not feel like I had to compromise those ideas. Here are the final two bullet points I could not agree with:

- I was a trainer and an equipper of students and believed this was the best way to reach lost students. My supervisor believed I should be a superstar youth pastor, able to reach every lost student on every high school campus. He thought I should spend more time going after the lost students, and I felt more time should be spent equipping students to reach their lost friends.
- I believed the primary focus of high school youth group needed to be the small group time students had with their leaders, where deeper conversations took place and trust was built. This part of our ministry was modeled after the church's small group ministry and functioned similarly to it. He believed the high school ministry should be a mini-church within our larger church, with me as the senior pastor. Therefore, its primary focus should be on the teaching/programming part of every Sunday night—the large group, fun event. On the surface, these may not seem like big differences, but with my boldness and desire for extra clarity, I realized just how far apart we were on these two bullet points.

Time was how I saw these differences come to life, specifically how I spent *my* time. I asked him the percentage of time he thought I should spend each week programming a "mini-church service" and going after the lost students. First, he answered that at least 70 percent of my time needed to be spent in the office, creating an attractional program every Sunday night. Second, I had small group leaders to spend time with their students, and I had adult coaches to invest in our small group leaders, so I should be going after not just lost students, but the most popular lost students. "If you get the captain of the football team, you get the whole team. If you get the captain of the cheerleading squad, you get the whole squad." And if I was the superstar youth pastor—or as we like to say today, "celebrity pastor"—all the students (adults) would be attracted to me and would want to come to youth group (church) because of me.

Consider the twelve disciples. Did Jesus enlist the most popular to get his message out? Did he recruit the Jewish teens who continued their Torah training and had already been discipled by a prominent rabbi? Or did he recruit the ones who barely made it through Torah school, the ones who were forced into their family's business because they barely passed their schooling . . . or even the ones who dropped out? These twelve disciples who changed the world came from low social status. Now, does that mean we neglect to reach out to those of the highest social status? Absolutely not! Luke writes his Gospel account and the book of Acts to Theophilus, who was of very high social standing and power within the Roman Empire.

Ultimately, we ended this conversation by agreeing to disagree. I was not going to spend the majority of my time creating an overtly attractive program. I was for sure not going to be the superstar youth pastor or the celebrity pastor of "my mini-church." He did not see the ministry being successful when I trained my small group leaders to be "youth pastors" for their students, equipping the students to be the best evangelists for their friends.

In the end, I realize methods are variable, even negotiable, but the mission should never change. We were both probably too strong-willed, too passionate about our methods. We both made the mistake of valuing our method over the mission.

For Clarity's Sake, You're Fired

It was a Friday, and my supervisor wanted the weekend to think about everything before coming back together on Tuesday to make a final decision.

Two days later was the last night of youth group of the spring semester. After this Sunday, we would have a few weeks off before we kicked off our summer programming in June. We honored our graduating seniors and had a big party to celebrate them. Throughout the night, I tried holding back the tears in every conversation I had with a leader or student. It was hard, knowing this would be the last time I would see many of these students in this context, but through the power of the Holy Spirit, I kept it together.

As I drove away from the church that night, I prayed that the Lord would give me compassion and grace when students and parents reached out to me after they found out I was leaving. I also prayed they would not hate the church or Jesus, but lean into Him more when learned I'd been fired (just as I had been doing).

The weekend passed, and Tuesday arrived. We entered our final meeting. Once again, I wanted to hear what my supervisor had to say. He was very diplomatic this time around. He said I was passionate and had deep convictions about ministry. He saw me as a "black and white" type of person but advised me I needed some more gray in my life to serve in ministry. Diplomacy aside, in his mind, I was stubborn. He didn't use that word, though, and I appreciated that. The CP asked him if he thought we could make this work, and he said he was leaning more toward no, but if he saw changes in me, he would give it a shot.

The question was directed at me, and I replied, "You've made it very clear over these past few weeks that I am not your guy for high school ministry, so go find your guy." Diplomacy aside, I was not going to sacrifice my family or compromise what I believed to be ministry essentials to work for him. It's probably best we each spoke honestly and directly because it allowed us to work through the final email to communicate with everyone. It had been nearly finalized a few weeks earlier, but we needed to make sure the three of us agreed on its content.

This was important because of the past "emails" that had been sent out about staff leaving or being fired. I wanted to make sure that my supervisor and the leadership took responsibility for the change in direction. Even though he did not want to say I was fired in the email, I made sure he communicated that I was not supporting this decision. It seemed like we were on the same page when we left the meeting—until later that day. My supervisor sent a "final draft" to only the CP, not me. I was intentionally left out of this "approval" email and had no idea of its existence.

The CP read it and was not happy with some of the language in it. I'd later learn a lot of back and forth via email happened in the next twenty-four hours because my supervisor was still trying to make it seem like my leaving was a mutual decision between us. Thankfully, the CP kept editing and re-editing the email that would be sent out to bring that message across. Even so, the email went out the next morning, and my supervisor completed it with his own edits, adding an extra paragraph that had not been reviewed by the CP. He used vague and confusing language that made it sound like it was a mutual decision, all without giving me the courtesy of reviewing what had been written—and not even knowing about the email exchanges. When I initially read the email, I was angry. But then, the Holy Spirit brought to mind Jesus's attitude when Pilate brought accusations from the crowd against Him. Jesus had been silent; He let the falseness and slander go; He confirmed that He was King, and He didn't let anyone else take away from His mission. So I surrendered to the same spirit that said, "Father, forgive them, for they don't know what they are doing" (Luke 23:24, NIV). It allowed me to find some peace for the rest of that day.

A Note to Leaders

Leaders, when you have to make this decision and, therefore, communicate this decision, pursue clarity and truthfulness. I'm not saying the communication has to include everything that happened with the employee you are firing but don't hide behind the tough decision you are making with confusing and vague language. As you will read in the next chapter, this confusion brought a lot of hurt to the people in our church. People will feel betrayed when a decision like this has to be made, but don't add to that hurt with confusion. Stand up for the tough decision you are making and be clear about why you believe it is in the best interest of your church. Finally, anytime in this chapter you saw the words employer, supervisor, or leader, I encourage you to go back and re-read that section. There is an abundance of applicable strategies for what to do and what not to do woven in and out of this part of my story. Please don't miss it.

6

HONESTY IS THE BEST POLICY

The controversial email was sent out on a Wednesday morning to parents and students in our church. I was asked to stay out of the office that entire morning so my supervisor could meet with various staff and break the news to them. I was with my wife, having an early lunch with a pastor and his wife from a church I was interviewing with when my phone blew up with messages. Though most students are not supposed to be on their phones at school . . . they're on their phones. Here are some texts I received:

- OMG! I'm so sad and am going to miss you so much!! I know you're not moving but I just meant like leaving the church. I'm so, so sad you were the best & I'm gonna miss all the fun times we had so much! Why didn't they let you stay any longer?
- I am VERY discouraged and confused as to why this decision was made. I just want to say that I am very

thankful for all that you've done and appreciate your heart to serve God. Thank you for genuinely caring for all of us by putting [in] the effort to get to know us and be involved in our lives. I pray and hope that this decision won't be final. You really display what it's like to live wholeheartedly for Him and that fellowship and a true relationship with God is what it's all about. You're the beeeeesssst! ☺

- I'M GONNA MISS YOU SO MUCH THIS STINKS!!! I've had 3 youth pastors and you have been the best one BY FAR; thanks so much for being the best person ever, I'm not sure how youth group is gonna function without you. This whole thing is so dumb I hate it!!"
- I want to say thank you for everything you've done for our youth group. You have no idea how much you mean to every student. I want you to know that we love you and we're not going down without a fight. I promise, we will be heard!

My heart broke as these texts flooded my phone while I was trying to engage in the interview process. The tension in my heart was heavy; just writing this part of the story brings tears to my eye. I cared so much about those students as they read this news for the *first time* . . . over an email or a text! I'd had almost six weeks to wrestle with this reality, so I put my heart and mind back to that first firing to remember the shock and empathize with the students. I allowed those emotions to fill my heart because what I really wanted to tell them was to get over it quickly. I had an interview (right then!), a job to secure, a family to provide for; I didn't have time to revisit this grief. I wanted the Band-Aid to be ripped off quickly, but also for my students to grieve and process properly. Instead, I had to remove it slowly, feeling the pain that I had initially felt when I first found out.

If you're in this place of getting fired and having people learn about it and contact you, let them grieve, let them get mad, let them vent. I know that is so difficult because you have to re-live all the reasons you think you should not have been fired, but don't miss this: God has called you to be their pastor for a bit longer, perhaps in one of the most important seasons yet.

God has called you to be their pastor for a bit longer, perhaps in one of the most important seasons yet.

As a pastor who counsels and cares for people, before you jump into "solution mode" for whatever it is they are struggling with, you must first listen, then grieve, empathize, and validate their feelings. Once you do that, they are more receptive to the wisdom and help you are offering them.

Love until It Hurts

I kept it together through the lunch interview, mainly because I didn't read through all the text messages or emails I received until lunch was over. But I spent the rest of that afternoon responding to people. I texted the various people, saying I was really sad too, that I loved them, and that if they wanted to meet for coffee, we could talk through why the leadership let me go. I chose not to explain anything electronically about my firing because I knew that could be interpreted a million different ways. It would be more beneficial for my students to meet with me face to face, even though I would have to engage in more tearful, painful conversations. Yes, it would've been easier to text back reasons, be vague, and not initiate conversation, but it's not about me. What will help that student, that person who just heard the news, is to represent Christlike kindness and care by having a personal conversation. *He* over *me*, no matter how much pain it brings back up in our hearts.

The CP and the junior high pastor told me not to come into the office but to work remotely because the environment held a mixture of tension and sadness. The overarching fear was "if someone so well-liked, a team player, and, from the outside, good at what he does was let go, it could happen to me anytime as well." The CP was a part of every "revelation" conversation with the staff and had multiple one-on-ones with staff in his office throughout the day to help them process the news.

As I responded to people that afternoon, I struggled with being honest without slandering my supervisor. The main idea we had agreed to share was that there was a "philosophy of ministry" difference in how to do student ministry—that was the phrase used in the email. In seminary, everyone has an idea of what this means, but the average church member has no idea, and after having multiple conversations with people, most couldn't care less about it. I communicated that I wanted to care more about leaders and students and my supervisor wanted me to focus more on developing an amazing program. Without saying those words, I also shared that my supervisor didn't want to neglect this care for students and leaders, and I didn't neglect to create a program, but the focus was shifting. For people who loved the programming *and* felt cared for by me, this was, as my students texted, "SO DUMB!!!"

without jumping onto my soapbox and screaming, "Yes!!! They are the micro-managers of all micro-managers!!! They are the least compassionate of all!!!" It was more like, "I am sorry you have seen this play out more than once; that saddens and hurts me as well." Second, I praised the Church—the capital "C" Church—the Church of every person who has put their faith in Jesus as their Savior. "Even though the leaders in this church have brought pain, just please do not give up on His Church. Whatever that looks like for your family, don't give up on the Church." Last, I encouraged a mutual pursuit of God. "God has been working in my heart as I continue to work through this pain; I hope you can lead your family in this same pursuit and grow closer to God through this situation too."

A couple of days later, there was a planned leader celebration for my adult leaders. My supervisor thought it would be appropriate for me to share with them what happened so "they wouldn't give up on the ministry." Though I agreed with this in the long run, I knew they were not in a place to hear "Don't give up on the ministry" a couple of days after hearing I was let go. I tried to explain this to my supervisor, as did the CP, but he said the only way I could attend this celebration without his attendance would be if I shared this message. I agreed and prepared for the agonizing conversation with my adult leaders.

As the evening meeting grew closer, I thought of Jesus's parable of the shrewd manager, found in Luke 16. I had read a book about being shrewd while in seminary, and it was the word the Lord kept impressing on my heart as I sat there with all of my leaders. This was supposed to be a celebration of God's work within the high school ministry over this past year—a huge appreciation extended to the volunteers for all of their hard work. Instead, it was a night filled with frustration, confusion, and sadness. How was I going to be shrewd in the way I shared? To define it more practically, how was I going to speak kindly about these difficult circumstances, as well as speak kindly about someone who had hurt me and, in my opinion, made a terrible decision to fire me? Even more so, how could I still encourage and celebrate with these leaders when the last thing anyone wanted was to be encouraged or celebrate? The timing of the communication and the way it was handled put us all in a tight spot.

I approached the meeting by choosing to lay out the timeline of events chronologically. I would talk about the month-and-a-half-long process, explaining why I had called a leader meeting on a Sunday night and then canceled it—because the leadership wanted more time to think through the decision. Then I wrote out this line, which I planned to communicate with the leaders: "After some in-depth conversations, the leadership made it clear, and I affirmed their clarity, that I was not the person to lead the ministry in the way they desired it to be led." I was intentional about affirming *only their clarity*, not affirming *their decision.*

When the time came, I could tell my leaders were still hurt and wanted more out of this meeting, out of me. They wanted to be mad and angry; they wanted to cry and voice their frustration over this all-too-familiar situation. Prior youth pastors were not fired but left for similar reasons, over similar conflicts with their leadership. I could also tell many of the leaders were done with serving, done with this church, and even done with ministry altogether. In the back of my mind, I heard my supervisor's words, directing me to tell them to keep serving. So I said, "I know you may feel like you're done right now, but your emotions are high, so don't make a decision either way. You need time and space and prayer to make this kind of decision about serving. You need to think about your role in your [small group] students' lives. Just like this ministry won't fall apart because one person is fired, your small group students won't hate Jesus because you leave. But if you stay, it will be a huge spiritual blessing for those hurting students. Please don't commit to anything tonight; don't make a decision until a significant amount of prayer goes into this decision, which means you may not make this decision until the end of the summer." In this, I was, with full integrity, able to tell my leaders to "not give up on the ministry." But that couldn't be the main thing or only thing I shared with them; that wouldn't be what was best for them in this moment of pain.

After I said what my supervisor wanted me to say, our time together shifted in a more positive direction. We shared some stories, and the leaders were so gracious to communicate what they appreciated most about what I had brought to the high school ministry for the past two years. We laughed; we cried, and we ended by praying and entrusting our students into the hands of a loving Father, who would always love them perfectly, even when His Bride did not act perfectly. We prayed that God would give wisdom to the leaders as they wrestled with Him in these upcoming summer months about their roles as leaders.

Drop the Gloves

Two days later, my leaders were invited to a meeting with my supervisor to talk about the transitions that would be taking place throughout the summer and the plan moving forward with the high school ministry. The meeting was supposed to be one hour long and between the Sunday morning services. It lasted just over three. The leaders tore to shreds every reason my supervisor used to let me go. Because I was not present at that meeting, I don't know firsthand what was said (though some of my leaders took detailed notes to make sure it was all recorded), but ultimately, I understand it turned ugly. Feelings were hurt, things were said about me that were not true—or a heavy exaggeration of the truth—and no one left that meeting feeling encouraged by the direction of the ministry, including my supervisor. In fact, he called me that afternoon. I did not answer. Then he texted me, telling me he believed I had not been honest with my leaders and if I could not communicate the same message he was, my severance would be in jeopardy. I immediately called the CP, who was at the meeting, read him the text, and he told me to block my supervisor's number from my phone. He would take care of it, and the three of us would discuss things on Tuesday, one of my last days in the office. I got off the phone, not knowing what was said in that meeting, but once again, feeling hurt, frustrated, and angry, assuming my supervisor had most likely slandered me, exaggerated my shortcomings, and then felt the need to threaten my severance.

When you get fired from a church, the unfortunate reality is that the neatly communicated, one-line reason never satisfies church members' hearts. Over the past few years, I have unfortunately encountered numerous pastors who have been let go; here are some of these "one-liners."

- "They were just not a good fit for what our church needs."
- "It is best for them to be at a different place in ministry."

- "This year's budget does not have room for their position."
- "We're Paul, and they're Barnabas, and we need to just go our separate ways."

I'm sure there are many others, but the one-liner method never satisfies minds and hearts. Out of a desire to protect the church leadership's reputation, the unfortunate default is to slander the pastor being fired. The justification is that they won't be around much longer, so it gives something tangible to the church attender that will answer their pointed questions and "satisfy" the questioner. Leadership tends to exaggerate truths, share only partial truths, or maybe even flat-out lie.

How do you "allow" these things to be said against you (because we can)? How do you avoid defending every false statement made against you (because we should)? How do you not go down the path of bitterness, rage, and hatred toward the church and your former supervisor (because we must)? Look to Jesus and His words: "But I say to you, love your enemies and pray for those who persecute you" (Matthew 5:44). Now that's a healthy one-liner!

We pray. We give these desires to God. We ask him to renew our hearts and give us the same love He has for our transgressors. If Jesus gave up His life for them, then we are called to do the same. Is it easy? Not at all! It's one of the hardest things to do, to love a follower of Jesus who has hurt you, who has torn you away from the people you dearly love. Yet as we pray, we choose not to respond to the slander(er). We choose to forgo whatever reputation we thought we had at that church and with the people we have cared for, and we leave it at the cross. Don't worry, our identity is not found in our reputations, anyway, so let it all go! In the same way Jesus stayed silent as the crowds and religious leaders hurled lies and insults at him on trial, we must stay silent. It is *not* our job to defend ourselves. *It is* our job to avoid engaging in any unwholesome talk that isn't encouraging to the body of believers.[9]

The following Tuesday, the three of us met for what felt like the thousandth time. My supervisor was not happy. He pressed into me about what I had shared on Friday. I told him what I had said, and he questioned my heart and my character and if I really wanted what was best for the high school ministry and the church. Even though I had said nothing untrue nor slandered him, I was once again under the threat of losing my severance and being questioned about my integrity. The CP intervened and explained to my supervisor that he had unrealistic expectations about the meeting on Sunday. There was no possible scenario where the volunteer leaders would be happy; no one in the high school ministry would've been happy, and he had sorely underestimated the impact I had on these leaders and families. He told him to allow people to be mad, to hurt, to grieve, and to give them the time they needed to process the information.

The CP also told us that the two of us needed to stop communicating with one another and any further communication between the two of us would require him to be present, copied on an email, or part of a group text. I was thankful to have the CP stand up for me; it made keeping my mouth shut a little bit easier!

The End of an Era

I was barely in the office during my final week of employment. I was allowed to meet with as many people as I wanted to, whenever

9 See Ephesians 4:29.

I wanted to, but outside of the office. Many students and parents met with my supervisor that week and after every meeting, they came to me with the same response: "It's as if he wasn't even listening to us," or "He was saying things that just weren't true of you." Even though everything inside of me wanted to get them on "my side," I chose empathy and sadness instead of doubling-down on sides. I would say things like, "I'm sorry that was a hard conversation for you and that it didn't bring clarity for you. I know I have felt that same way in these last couple of months. As hard as it is, I know God loves you and will be there for you, as He has been there for me in these days and weeks. And however I can be there for you, I will be there for you too." I would focus on their needs and frustrations, allowing myself to slowly pull off that Band-Aid of pain to care for them. I chose to be their pastor because when your "sheep" are going through a difficult time,they need their "shepherd" to care for them.

The momentary "feel good" of vomiting all of your problems at people's feet, those who are seemingly ready to hear from you, can do greater damage to them and bring more confusion and hurt than the firing itself.

As I have written before, it is easier to share everything with those around you because that is what feels good to you. If you get it off your chest, you'll get them on your side, and they will dislike your "enemy." It is a personal victory at the expense of the church. The momentary "feel good" of vomiting all of your problems at people's feet, those who are seemingly ready to hear from you, can do greater damage to them and bring more confusion and hurt than the firing itself.

Maybe you've seen this play out before in a kids' classroom; one little kid gets sick and throws up all over the floor. Within a few seconds, there's another kid who sees and smells the vomit, and his or her gag reflex kicks in—vomit everywhere, again! This is why you need someone in there who doesn't have the gag reflex to get all the kids out before it happens again. This is also why you need someone to clean up the mess who doesn't have the gag reflex.

Most people, even church members, have a gag reflex. If you vomit, they will vomit even more. If you share your frustrations with one or two people, they will share it with five or six. Don't be a vomit-enabler; be a vomit-preventer (not sure if those count as words, but you get the picture, though maybe you didn't want this vomit picture in the first place—my apologies). I had students, parents, and leaders who continued to press me for details, trying to make sense of everything, not fully understanding why this decision was made. Confusion was the normal response from most people who talked to my supervisor in the month after my firing was made public. But instead of sharing my hurts and pains, I shared with them *in their hurts and pains*. Instead of vomiting all over the place, I kept their gag reflex down and gave them the medicine of love, listening, grieving, and compassion. I kept them pointed to the Great Physician, the only one who could truly heal us in this difficult situation.

Honesty vs. Completely Honest

It was a little easier to be honest with everyone because, in a sense, I had practiced or prepared a month ago with my family and a few close staff members. For most people, you won't get this practice, but I want to encourage you to still pursue this type of honesty and attitude when people from your church ask you questions about your firing. In the immediate, it might feel good to share anything and everything with everyone, to be "completely honest." You can still be honest without slandering; it is nearly impossible to be *completely* honest without slandering. Most likely, you had been pretty good at withholding conflict, dissension, and other challenges from people before you were fired. Don't take this opportunity to go backward. Speak the truth in love, and by "love" I mean, when you speak, don't say anything unloving about your supervisor or the church leadership. It will not help the people in your church, and it will make you feel more discouraged about the entire situation. As that friend from church said a few days after the first firing, they don't want to hear it all because it can corrupt their minds and hearts toward the Church. Choose to protect Christ's Bride over protecting your status and reputation with those in your church.

A Different Kind of Note

In lieu of the "Note to the Leader" section, I want to take a moment and address a prevalent issue in the Church. Real quick though: Leaders, don't be surprised when people question your decision; don't be surprised when people become upset, even if it is only a few people. Speak honestly without being completely honest because when we get into completely honest, it gets blurred with our opinions, which are not Gospel truths.

OK, back to a different kind of note: As I talk about not being "completely honest," there is a time for a staff person to be "completely honest." It is when they are facing issues of any type of abuse. I have thought a lot about my firing. I've talked extensively with the CP over the years (he still meets regularly with me to counsel and encourage me in life and ministry), and I would say that even though I never felt spiritually or emotionally abused by my supervisor, there are still many people who do experience abuse as they go through their firing experience.

What's the difference? To be honest, it is a gray line, and I am not an expert in deciding where that line sits. However, I have researched this subject in detail and want to recommend a couple of resources to you if you haven't listened to or read these already.[10]

One definition I resonated with is from Scot McKnight's blog post on Christianity Today's website. He writes, "Spiritual abuse is a form of emotional and psychological abuse. It is characterized by a systematic pattern of coercive and controlling behavior in a religious context. Spiritual abuse can have a deeply damaging impact on those who experience it. This abuse may include manipulation and exploitation, enforced accountability, censorship of decision-making, requirements for secrecy and silence, coercion to conform, [inability to ask questions], control through the use of sacred texts or teaching, requirement of obedience to the abuser, the suggestion that the abuser has a

10 "The Rise and Fall of Mars Hill." Podcast produced by Christianity Today, 2021. McKnight, Scot, and Laura Barringer. 2020. *A Church Called Tov: Forming a Goodness Culture That Resists Abuses of Power and Promotes Healing*. Tyndale House Publishers, Inc. Oakley, Lisa, and Justin Humphreys. 2019. *Escaping the Maze of Spiritual Abuse: Creating Healthy Christian Cultures*. SPCK.

'divine' position, isolation as a means of punishment, and superiority and elitism."[11]

As I go through this list of "inclusions," I do not find myself in any of these categories. Though my supervisor and I had our disagreements, and though I felt he lacked empathy toward me and handled the communication of my firing poorly, this would not (in my mind) be classified as abuse. Mismanagement? Absolutely. But not abuse.

I have heard from ministry staff around the country about their experiences, and they could resonate with some of the descriptors listed by McKnight. In fact, some staff experienced this abuse before being fired or forced to resign; it got so toxic and abusive that they willingly chose to leave. I write all this to say that if you find yourself in this type of situation—of being abused—you need to be "completely honest." This is not a time to leave silently to protect the Bride and care for the sheep. At first, this does not mean you tell the whole church and blast the leadership on your social media accounts. But you should go to your supervisor's boss, most likely a church board member (an elder, deacon, etc.), and be completely honest with them. If they are not willing to address it or lead any type of investigation or offer mediation with your supervisor, you should look to leave as soon as you can. Unfortunately, many abused staff do not get the opportunity to "leave on their own."

To be clear, my story and this book are not about abusive situations. As I have already shared in the footnotes, there

---

11 McKnight, Scot. "What Is 'Spiritual' Abuse? A Working Definition." December 2, 2020. From Jesus Creed Blog on www.christianitytoday.com.

are great resources to listen to or read, which can help you process this pain and give you practical next steps to take, sometimes even legal steps. We have seen many churches (Evangelical, Anglican, Roman Catholic, Southern Baptist, etc.) be refined these last five years when church staff leave and call out the abusive leadership. There are many stories of church abuse survivors who have come out on the other side stronger and more like Jesus, despite what has been done to them. If you're there, be completely honest and seek the help that you need.

7

CH-CH-CHANGES

I cleaned out my office on that Friday morning, a week and a half after everyone learned of my firing. With the last couple of boxes of books in my arms, I headed to my car. As I was walking out the doors, a shiny reflection caught my eye. I saw underneath a couch in our lobby a McDonald's gift card. I picked it up and drove to the McDonald's that was on my way home from church. I went in and told the cashier, "I found this gift card and don't know how much is on it. It might be empty, or it could have $200 or more on it." He cracked a smile and checked. "Almost $200, indeed—only about $195 short. Almost!" His smile widened. Five dollars was all I needed for a timeless order, an order I had made numerous times as a college student but had forgotten since my metabolism slowed down soon after graduating: two cheeseburgers, a large fry, and a large Coke.

As I sat there in the McDonald's café, eating my comfort food, I reminisced about my college years, specifically those late-night McDonald's runs during my senior year, when I was engaged to my wife without a clue what I would do after I graduated from Bible college. I was knee-deep in sending out resumes and looking for a job in ministry. There was a self-imposed pressure to find something sooner rather than later because I did not want to spend the first few months of marriage living in my parent's basement, and neither did my soon-to-be wife. It's that millennial complex; I can't escape it! I remembered how the Lord provided for my wife and me that summer. By August of that same year, we had an apartment; she was working at a university, and I was a full-time youth pastor. If God was faithful six years ago to provide, my McDonald's miracle that day was a subtle reminder that He was going to be faithful again in this new season of unknowns and many changes.

Sometimes, God blesses us in the most unusual of ways. In those moments of unexpected blessings, He speaks kindly to us, reminding us He is with us, will never leave us, and has a plan and purpose for our lives that is bigger and better than we could ever imagine. If you find yourself forced into a new season of unknowns, it's easy to look for the *grandiose* ways God can bless and provide for you, specifically by finding a new job. But don't miss out on the small things, the ways God cares for you that you may take for granted—or sometimes used to take for granted in the past when the *bigger* blessings filled your life. I don't know how that gift card ended up underneath that couch, but it was the reminder I needed that God was with me. It was the small, weird McDonald's miracle that I won't forget. Anytime I see a McDonald's gift card in a store, I am reminded of God's faithfulness to me. I might be the only person on the planet who sees that as a blessing. I know—it's weird. But I'm not going to forget God's faithfulness to me unless McDonald's goes out of business. And I'm sure Jesus will return before that happens!

The truth is God provided in some bigger ways as well, and as I type these words, tears are welling in my eyes. There were two *grandiose* ways God provided within this trial. The first was with time, and the second involved finances. I don't know how God is going to tangibly provide for you in your trial, but He will provide. Many times, He will bless and provide through His people and His Church, His Beautiful Bride. That's why it is so important to not lead those people down a path of negativity because they might be the people God uses to care for you as you navigate your fire(d) trial.

The Blessings of Change

My wife was still going to doctor's appointments multiple times a week, but now, I could go to all of them and still be at home to help take care of our kids. There was no rushing, no trying to beat traffic. A new calmness and rhythm permeated our lives. My severance lasted until the end of June, almost seven weeks of continued paychecks and insurance. After only six years of working in full-time ministry, it was as if I had earned a sabbatical a year early! Merry Christmas to me! As a dad with two kids, I cherished every moment with my family. Though some parts were hard and exhausting, it was still great for our family to be at home—together. What a tremendous blessing from God to get paid to take care of my wife and kids without the pressure of feeling I was missing out on my job.

I still carried the weight of actively pursuing opportunities because July 1 was coming whether or not I had a new job. And with these interviews, meetings, and meet and greets, there were times

I had to be away from my family. Thankfully, many of my former leaders and even some families from the church made us meals, watched the kids while I was gone, and even gave my wife and me an hour to ourselves by watching our kids from time to time. One of the volunteer leaders gifted his tithe to me until I found a new job. He wanted to make sure that we never missed a mortgage payment. I'm not sure if that's what a tithe is for, but he told me "One way or another, my tithe is going to pay for someone's salary at the church, so I'm just now designating it to you!" I'd have to dig deeper before recommending this to anyone, but he was convinced this was what God wanted him to do. How could I argue with his generosity?

My "old" church was still caring for us; it was bittersweet for sure, but we were grateful for their tremendous kindness to us. Once again, care for your sheep; protect your sheep from negativity because when you're hurting, your sheep will care for you.

My "sabbatical" was such a blessing, and within that time, the Lord provided (as LeBron would say) "Not one, not two, not three, not four . . ."—OK, maybe just three—but *three* local church opportunities to be a youth pastor. Throughout April and into May, I was having multiple interviews with these three churches in the area, each no more than a thirty-minute drive from home. Knowing that moving was not an option, I could not believe the Lord had provided three different opportunities to work at churches as a youth pastor! On the three consecutive Sundays following Mother's Day, we attended each of these churches and lunch afterward so the staff and leaders could meet my wife and get to know me better. Every week, my kids were taken care of by family and friends after church so Maria and I could interview and talk with the church leaders.

By the middle of June, my wife and I had made our decision. We accepted the position at a church located even closer to our home than our previous church. We once again saw God's providence and provision in this season. A year before, my wife and I had purchased our current home, but not without any difficulties. When we began our search, many of the homes we looked at were west and north of our church. This is where our previous apartment was located; this was where many of our students were going to school; this was the center of our church community. However, we put offers on six different houses and were out-bid on every single offer . . . and it wasn't even the summer of 2021—the sellers' boom!

It was a discouraging time, but we finally looked at a couple of houses that were southeast of our church. It was a little outside of the community our church was reaching, but it was still close enough to be only a fifteen- or twenty-minute drive. The one house in this area we put an offer on was well within our price range, but we had grown weary because we figured a bidding war would ensue. However, the homeowner was ready to sell and sold immediately! We looked at the house the first day it was on the market and put in an offer that night. The owner only negotiated with us. She canceled the showings scheduled over the next few days, and within twenty-four hours, she accepted our offer! Unheard of! Little did we know, just a year later, this house would be in our new church's surrounding community and even closer than our old church. Buying any house west and north of our old church would have made all three new opportunities difficult to manage. But God knew, God provided . . . God was faithful once again.

I don't know how God is going to show His faithfulness to you as you leave your church and enter into this new season. He may provide a church for you to be at immediately and reaffirm the calling He has put on your life to be in ministry. He may call you into the secular world before calling you to serve in full-time church ministry again later. He may not provide something for a while and instead, you might work at temporary jobs for a season. Whatever happens, look for those small, weird blessings during this trial. Just because He hasn't provided you with something immediately does not mean He has forgotten you. Most likely, it is a call to lean into Him more, to find your identity and contentment in Him—not in serving Him, not in serving and leading His people, not in making a decent living and providing for your family (all of which are good), but in Him. That whole "wait on the Lord" thing we preach about, we, too, have to put into practice! Yet it is so worth it as we become more like Jesus and represent Him to those around us.

If you find yourself in this refined by the fire(d) season and need extra support in finding help and healing, discerning what's next, or networking, I would encourage you to check out Pastor's Hope Network. This organization was founded with the purpose of helping church staff members that have been forced to resign or terminated from their ministry positions. They offer various counseling and career services that can be helpful for you as you pursue what's next for your calling and career in life. Find out more about them at www.pastorshopenetwork.org.

New Season, New Trials

God had provided for us in tremendous ways during my "sabbatical," but we were still being refined by fire(d), even in a new church. We entered a whole new aspect of this trial that neither of us expected. The Lord was going to use it to make us more like Jesus. As God was faithful in those seven weeks, He would be faithful to accomplish His purposes in my life, especially in this new season ahead.

There was a sense of excitement in my home as I got ready for my first day in the office at our new church. We had spent the previous two Sundays there, attending and getting to know people. The student pastor at this church was leaving to pursue a year-long leadership program on the other side of the country with the goal of becoming an executive pastor someday. He had been at this church for five years; he was not being pushed out but choosing to leave. He had his frustrations with things, but as we all know, there will always be frustrations at any church; the grass is never greener, as they say. He was gracious to share those frustrations, but ultimately, he was optimistic and encouraged me in my new role. He was celebrated as he left, and I was coming in to continue moving the student ministry in a healthy direction. My wife knew I was excited about this opportunity and as much as she loved having me at home every day, she knew this was God's plan to continue to provide for us in this season of our lives.

As I pulled up to the church offices that morning, there was one car in the parking lot. The office manager was the only person there the entire day! She helped me get my keys, computer, and other things set up, but other than that, there was minimal interaction. It was July 5, so everyone was on vacation, extending the long weekend into a week's vacation. My only appointment that day was meeting my new supervisor, the executive pastor who had hired me, for lunch. I spent most of the day cleaning and organizing my office: moving furniture, hanging pictures, getting desk supplies, and putting books on bookshelves—all normal, first-day things. However, that morning, I was caught off-guard as I was swept under some deep, dark emotions that seemingly hit me out of nowhere. I realized I was lonely and sad, and I began to cry as the reality sunk in that I had been fired and was now restarting ministry life. I thought I had spent the last two months working through these emotions, so why was I feeling this way on my first day?

Well, I would feel this way almost every day for the entire summer and even into the fall. I felt myself longing for my old relationships, missing the other students, families, and staff. Every day—no exaggeration—I had to give myself a pep talk to get out of my office and engage in conversations with my new co-workers. Every Sunday was a struggle *to want to* get to know new students and families. Even with the student trips planned for the summer, I dreaded them because I would have to spend quality time with new people. I didn't get it; this wasn't who I was or who I'd ever been. I am *the* extrovert of extroverts, but all I wanted to do was hide.

In those first few months, there were two things I really struggled with and my guess is, whenever you start a new position at a church or get back into attending/serving at a church, you might struggle with these two things too: connection and comparison. I'll get to comparison a bit later, but the issue I am describing above will be the first one you have to work through: *connection.*

Connection

Connection is something everyone needs, from acquaintances to deep intimacy with Jesus and everyone in between. We all need to be connected with other humans; it's how God created us to function, from "in the beginning" to right now, and into eternity.

What can make connecting difficult is having to start new connections over and over again. When entering a season of life where you have to make new connections, it is nice to have those old, deeper connections close by to help you through it. But in the church world, when those deeper connections are usually from people within your church, you don't have them anymore. As pastor and leader Carey Nieuwhof wrote, "I realized that ministry combines three areas of life that are intensely personal. Ministry combines your faith, your work and your community. Because of that, what you do is what you believe, what you believe is what you do and your friends are also the people you serve and lead. Throw your family into the mix (because they believe what you believe and are friends with the people you/they lead and serve) and *bam*—it's even more jumbled."[12] When you are most hurting and in need, you realize you most likely don't have your closest relationships to turn to for support and encouragement; and your family doesn't have them either.

When you are most hurting and in need, you realize you most likely don't have your closest relationships to turn to for support and encouragement; and your family doesn't have them either.

Now, I understand that not everyone who starts a new church position has the luxury of still being in the same home and close proximity to so many people. Since we did, I assumed

12 Nieuwhof, Carey. "The Affair You Are Most Likely To Have as a Christian Leader." December 2022. www.careynieuwhof.com.

we would stay close, maintaining that connection we had built up over the past two years and especially relied on during the beginning months of the summer. Unfortunately, that wasn't the case for the majority of those connections. Once people found out I had started at a new church, they congratulated me, but then there was little to no contact with them. I was in a new place, and they could go back to their lives in their church community. The few people that we still connected with were processing their own frustrations, thinking through their "what is our next step" at the church, because they were still hurting, still grieving.

At my new church, I found myself not wanting to open up with people immediately. I was reserved and didn't openly share my thoughts on staff-wide discussions. Instead, I enjoyed hiding in my office, alone. I realized I was protecting myself from any conflict or disagreement because I had lost all sense of freedom and safety with my previous church experience. To top it all off, as the student pastor, I was overseeing a thirty-hour-per-week student ministry director. I had to be a supervisor, the boss, and I was scared.

One reason I took this new position was because I wanted to do things "right" as a supervisor. My former supervisor did everything "wrong" (not really, but I still felt that way). But I wanted to make sure I was not like him and do everything "right." That's a lot harder than I thought, especially when in the first couple of months, I didn't want to connect with the student director. Not because he was awful; he was personable, helpful, and encouraging. I just didn't want to connect with anyone!

Losing old connections and struggling to make new connections . . . it was my story and my wife's story in those first few months. The people from our old church had to continue living their already busy lives; they had to continue investing in their church family, their community, and even a new high school pastor (more on that in a bit). There was no margin in their lives to continue to invest in us when we were no longer in close proximity to them on a consistent basis.

On the flip side, the people in our new church welcomed us with open arms. Living in close proximity to our old church, many people from our new church knew people from our old church. One of the most common things I heard in the first few months from people from our new church was, "I'm not sure why you're not there anymore, but we are glad you are here! (Insert the name of the person from the old church) talks about how awesome you and your family are!" Instead of being thankful for this warm welcome and "positive gossip" being spread about me, I longed for those who had no time for me and emotionally pushed away those who had plenty of time for me.

Why Does It Have to Be This Way?

This was my struggle, and it might be your struggle as you start over with a new church. There's a part of you that longs for those previous relationships, but there is also the excitement of connecting with new people who don't know the full *you* yet, just the good parts of you. It's like the person who is dating for the first time after ending a long-term relationship. You miss the comfort and security of that former relationship, but the prospect of finding someone new is exciting! I was excited to meet new people, but I didn't realize how hard it would be to emotionally and spiritually invest in new people at a new church. It would take time, energy, sacrifice, and love, all of which I felt like I had very little of in this new season. The best piece of wisdom I learned that helped with this tension came through Paul's letters to different churches.

Paul always mentioned different people when he ended one of his letters to a specific church. In his last three epistles in our Bibles, 1 and 2 Timothy and Titus, he mentions thirty-four different people from those churches he helped to start. In Acts 20:13–36, he has a heartfelt departure from the elders in Ephesus. Paul had connections, yet, as a missionary, he was called to go from one city to the next to spread the gospel. Did Paul miss his old connections? Absolutely! He loved those people! But the calling on his life to spread the Gospel was greater than his heart to shepherd and care for the churches in which he was their spiritual father. In a similar way, God had called me, and maybe He will call you, to be in a new place to spread the Gospel.

Our "God is calling me" paths might look different from Paul's. He was never technically "fired," but there were some tumultuous circumstances that caused his departure. Yet those circumstances were not a shock to the God who is sovereign over all. Paul knew that all too well: "And we know that for those who love God, all things work together for good, for those who are called according to his purpose" (Romans 8:28). All things, including being fired, will work together for God's purpose in your life and mine to spread His Gospel. In our pursuit of doing this, God will create connections with the new people we are shepherding. Like Paul, we will have lists of names of the people from our past church, but we will also have many new names of people at our next church. Does it take time? Yes! But when we ask God daily to heal our hurts and open our hearts to new connections, He will be faithful to do so like he did for Paul.

Change Is Good

Surprisingly, there is a benefit from losing the intimacy of most of those old connections; it keeps you (mostly) out of the old church drama. In my experience, when a staff person gets fired, people within the church will choose sides. Maybe there are exceptions to this, but I have seen this unfortunate reality play out over and over again because churches are full of sinful people, myself included! Our tendency is to want to find fault when something happens. Though our job is to not cause division or put blame on our leadership when we are fired, it will sometimes happen. Our actions within the revelation can cause the fall-out to be minimal, but it will happen. And those who were on "your side" will keep you updated about their issues with the church.

Over those first few months, anytime my wife or I would see those "on our side" connections from our old church, the conversation somehow always steered toward the things they didn't like about the church. It was as if they needed someone to vent to who they felt could relate to their issues. At first, I felt a sense of pride—that once again I was right, and my supervisor had been wrong. Even some pride-filled thankfulness came over me, kind of like the Pharisee in Luke 18, who prayed out loud that he was so thankful to God that he was not like the evil people of his day. However, the Holy Spirit quickly convicted me of these prideful feelings, and through His strength, I would try to change the subject, saying I was sorry they were still struggling as I had been in the past.

This became especially poignant when former students still wanted to meet me for coffee or lunch. Since they were high school students, they were always willing to drive to meet me. It made it even easier to meet with them since our time together was about how the high school ministry had changed, and they didn't like it or how they didn't like the new high school pastor (talk about a pride-fueler) or whatever else they were frustrated with at the church. My pride loved hearing the youth group had shrunk to nearly half the size it was when I left.

I soon realized I was still longing for these old connections so that I *could feed my pride*, not because I cared about these people, who I was not loving well as brothers and sisters in Christ. I was being selfish, and I knew I could not engage in these conversations anymore. Since I was the one who was mostly pursuing these old connections, I stopped pursuing them and started focusing on connecting with new people, leaders, families, and students at my new church.

And just like with the adult connections, my pride needed to be killed with my youth group connections. The best way for something to be killed is to deprive it of nutrition; don't feed the beast of pride. As hard as this was, I had to limit my face-to-face interactions with my students.

That shift was life-giving!

I found myself thinking about and praying more for my new connections than for my old connections. It took about three or four months, but my heart and mind slowly changed. And, I realized, most of those old connections weren't pursuing connection with me anymore too. And the few who did, my wife and I still connect with them to this day, and the conversations are never about anything negative about the old church.

Killing Comparison

Even though the connections decreased, there was still a strong, unhealthy desire for comparison that was leading to jealousy in my heart. Comparison was one thing I did not think would be a big struggle for me until I got into my new ministry. I think this is the one that many fired staff will struggle with in their new church. We compare every aspect of our new church with our old church, sometimes without even realizing it, and that can be deadly to living how God has called us to live.

I compared the staff culture, my relationship with my supervisor, the type of connection I had with my senior pastor, the people within the church, the working environment within the office—the list went on and on. I was playing the "grass *is* (or should be) greener over here" game. Everything at my new church was way better and *everything* my old church did was terrible.

I struggled with this mindset quite often, but over time, the Lord revealed to me that this thinking was destructive. I never verbalized these thoughts, but they would replay in my head like some inner critic. Once I recognized these comparison thoughts, I knew I had to dispel them quickly, and I asked God to help me remove them. I wanted to dwell on the good happening in my church. Throughout this process, God filled my mind with good thoughts and gratitude for what I had experienced and learned in my old church. And some of those things were helpful for leading in my new church.

Another part of killing my pride and avoiding comparison was disabling my social media accounts. As a millennial, I engaged in all the platforms and used them daily. Even though I stopped the face-to-face interactions, I was still connected online because I followed people from my old church. This ongoing connection kept my heart tethered and in a bad place. I would see their posts and long to be a part of their lives again. I still followed the high school ministry and the church's Instagram accounts and felt myself falling into (wait for it) the *comparison trap.* Yes, even church leaders struggle with this in ministry. The envy and longing intensified in my heart because I wanted to have better events, better posts, and better "results" on social media than my old ministry. It was foolish and prideful and brought me to a place of frustration, anger, and resentment often.

The only solution was to get rid of all my social media accounts; I deleted and deactivated (destroyed) all of them. This was a hard decision for me because I knew I would miss out on some aspects of people's lives moving forward. I still wanted to see my family's updates, specifically cousins and extended cousins, whom I had better stayed connected with because of social media. I had connected with friends at my first church located an hour away from where we lived, friends from college, friends from high school, and even people from my new church—all of which I would lose (at least the social media connection). I knew this might mean losing a significant connection with them in every way. I'm not anti-social media;

I think it's a good thing that helps people stay connected. As long as it's used in moderation, I find it very beneficial, but I couldn't do it because my heart needed to be cleaned of anger, pride, and comparison.

Embracing the Changes

Wherever you are at in your fire(d) season, a few months in or even a couple of years down the road, finding good connections in your new church community, whether you are simply attending or on staff, and avoiding the comparison game will help you thrive where God has placed you. With anything new comes good and challenging aspects. God wants to bring so much good into your life when you work through the challenges of making new connections, losing the intimacy of old connections, and removing the thoughts of constant comparison from your new church to your old. But don't shy away from your thoughts and feelings; hold them captive and ask the Lord to make your thoughts like His thoughts for His church. He's put amazing people in your life to connect with and care for in the same way He connects and cares for His people. He isn't comparing one of His churches to another. He loves them all equally, no matter how broken they are, and we should too!

Paul writes we should "be transformed by the renewing of our minds" (Romans 12:2b, NIV). In our context, it means thinking about the Church as a whole (capital *C*) and not as individual churches. It also means viewing the people in the Church as not being confined to a specific church location but everyone as a part of one big family. With this thinking, there's no need to compare because we are all a part of God's Church! On the other side, there's no need to withhold ourselves from connecting with others because the one thing that can and will bind us forever is that we are all children of the one true God. When we take on this God-sized thinking about the church, comparison and connection issues will dwindle.

This new season of ministry will hopefully challenge you, as it did me. But I hope you see these trials and challenges as a blessing from God who will change the way you think about church ministry forever.

A Note to Leaders

After reading this far, maybe you're at a place right now of feeling guilty or regretful for your decision to fire a staff member. If that's the case, I want to encourage you to pursue, as Paul writes, "godly sorrow" (2 Corinthians 7:10, NIV). This is not a time to beat yourself up and feel ashamed for past mistakes; that is shame, and Satan wants that for you. This is a time to ask God to forgive you for your shortcomings, humble yourself before Him, and see how you can act and lead differently. I believe God can and will redeem a poor staffing decision just like He did in my life.

In Paul's letter, this godly sorrow brings "salvation and leaves no regret." He's writing specifically about the salvation we receive in Christ alone, but I think this principle can apply to us. We can experience a new type of life, a new way of living (leading), being saved and redeemed from our old life and the old way of living (leading). We don't have to regret the past poor decision; we can make the changes needed to be the best leaders for our staff moving forward. If you're still in leadership, believe that God will give you another opportunity to experience redemption in leading staff. Believe that God is already redeeming the life and ministry of that staff member who you didn't get it right for the first time. He's bigger than all of our failures and shortcomings and is an expert in redeeming human brokenness.

8
TRUST THE PROCESS

Joel Embiid, a professional basketball player for the Philadelphia 76ers, became widely known for emphasizing the phrase "trust the process." He repeated it throughout his first few seasons in the NBA when his team was terrible and he sat out because of injury. After a few years of constant misery and consistent losing, Embiid stayed healthy, and the team started winning. At this point, they have not won a championship, but the "process" of being terrible, securing top talent in the draft, waiting for players to get healthy, and then winning, is finally working. Though the "process" to become a competitive team took a long time to unfold, the "process" has seemingly paid off. All along, Embiid kept telling everyone to "trust the process." Meaning? Though we are terrible now, we will be better soon!

After moving on, whether into a new career or a new place in ministry, I hoped I would forget about the hurt and pain that season of life caused—forever! However, that was not the case. I found as time went on, I struggled with many other thoughts and feelings that were not present during and soon after the firing. Through this, I realized the Lord had more for me. He had a process of refining me in the fire(d), making me more like Jesus, and it wasn't just within my firing. I had to *trust this process* of continuing to work on the things the Lord wanted to rid me of in my heart and mind.

My guess is that He has the same long road for many of you. There are certain things I struggled with and needed to work on in the long term that are probably similar to the things God wants to work out inside you. I will list five in this chapter. They are interconnected and deal with our minds and hearts. They are internal struggles, independent of what anyone says or does to you, but all dependent on what goes on inside you. The Lord wants to transform you and make you more like Jesus . . . and that takes time! It's a process, so trust it. Here's what the Lord was doing in me as He kept me in the refined by fire(d) process.

Wrestling with Anger

From the first firing through the first couple of months in my new job, I was never angry with God. I clearly saw how God was providing for my family in a variety of ways. But once those provisions lost their "newness," I grew bitter. I was angry at God for removing me from my previous job and from the relationships at my old church I cherished. I no longer compared myself or longed for those connections; I was just mad about them. I woke up daily feeling angry and frustrated with God about how He'd moved me and planted me in this new season of life.

My attitude reminded me of the Israelites in Numbers 14. Moses had sent twelve spies into the Promised Land to scope it out. All of Israel knew God was going to give them this land, and He had already shown them His miraculous and loving power and care (parting the Red Sea, providing manna and quail, bringing forth water from a rock). Yet when ten of the twelve spies reported that the Promised Land was filled with giants, that the Israelites would have no chance of defeating their enemy, the Israelites got angry and frustrated at God.

> *Then all the congregation raised a loud cry, and the people wept that night. And all the people of Israel grumbled against Moses and Aaron. The whole congregation said to them, "Would that we had died in the land of Egypt! Or would that we had died in this wilderness! Why is the Lord bringing us into this land, to fall by the sword? Our wives and our little ones will become a prey. Would it not be better for us to go back to Egypt?" And they said to one another, "Let us choose a leader and go back to Egypt"* (Numbers 14:1–4).

They wanted to go back, not only through the wilderness but back to Egypt, subjecting themselves to slavery. They were ready to throw out God's appointed leaders and pick their own to lead them back into bondage. In essence, they told God, "You got it wrong. We're angry at you, so we are going to take things into our own hands." Sadly, that Israelite generation never got to experience the Promised Land because they pushed away the process God had asked them to endure to increase their faith and dependence on Him.

This is what I was doing. I was mad at God for having to leave my old church. I had not forgotten how God brought my wife and me to a healthy place in ministry; I had not forgotten about the freedom and flexibility I was being afforded so I could still take care of my injured wife; I had not forgotten about the way this new church welcomed and loved my family. But I still just wanted to be back at my old church, and I was mad that God had removed me.

Our feelings are valid and real but don't always align with God's best. It was illogical for both the Israelites and me to feel the way we did, especially since we all recalled God's faithfulness. Being angry with the One who has proven His faithfulness and love makes no sense. Yet, there I was, feeling mad. And my guess is on some days, you feel that way too. Maybe not every day, but once a week, every month, once in a while, anger and frustration are heaped up toward God: "God, why are you bringing me into this land?" It's in these moments of frustration that we have to make the conscious decision to thank God for His past provision and trust Him in the present testing.

I went back and reminded myself of the things I "knew" God had done in the past. Whether it was re-reading old journal entries or verbally thanking God for how He had provided, I had to be disciplined to show Him gratitude for past provisions. But I couldn't just stop there; I had to thank Him for the process too. Specifically, the process of being refined and removing the anger in my heart through confession and repentance. He was revealing to me that my anger toward Him was rooted in my pride, that I thought I knew what was best for my life, not Him. He reminded me I'm not Him, and I can't think like Him or know what He knows.

Making the commitment to thank God for past provisions and present testing helped the anger in my heart toward God subside. There are still moments when I can feel that anger in my heart, but I've gotten better at quickly moving to a place of gratitude. Is it easy? Nope. Not even now. But I've had a lot of practice—especially in that first year. By trusting the process and choosing gratitude for God's work in my past and present, my anger at God has dropped away and my trust in Him has been renewed and squashed the prideful trust I had in myself.

Choosing Forgiveness

It was almost like clockwork: as I worked through dealing with my anger against God, that anger would transfer over toward someone from my old church. Sometimes it was directed at my supervisor for the way he unfairly treated me; sometimes it was feeling like people at my old church had forgotten me or stopped caring about my family. Other times I became angry at some of my previous leaders, who stuck with the high school ministry and continued serving. Some of my anger may have been justified in the sense that my supervisor brought pain into my life, but so much of it was unfounded and harmful to my heart.

I quickly realized I had to choose forgiveness. The more I dwelled on how this person hurt me or how I felt neglected or betrayed, the harder it was to get out of the angry, frustrated, and ultimately sinful mindset. I concluded that if God was willing to forgive them and not hold anything against them because of

Jesus, then I had to do the same. These words of Jesus really stood out to me in this season of struggling to forgive: "For if you forgive others their trespasses, your heavenly Father will also forgive you, but if you do not forgive others their trespasses, neither will your Father forgive your trespasses" (Matthew 6:14–15). If I continued to withhold forgiveness, how could God forgive me? I know this verse can be taken out of context because, in Christ, we have complete eternal forgiveness. So if we can't forgive right away, it doesn't mean we don't have full forgiveness before God. However, this perspective from Dr. Michael Vanlaningham, in his commentary on Matthew, was helpful as I worked through my unforgiving heart:

> *It is better to see it as indicating that one's capacity for forgiving others is tied to the receipt of forgiveness from God. If one does not or cannot forgive others, it may indicate that he has not yet received forgiveness, so forgiving others becomes evidence of one's forgiveness before God.*[13]

The choice you and I make to forgive those who have hurt us is a clear indication that we have experienced complete forgiveness in Christ. The daily decision to say, "I forgive you" is a great reminder of God's forgiveness toward you. As people who have been fired from a ministry position, we need to cling to God's grace and forgiveness as our source for showing that same forgiveness. In the same way God forgives us daily for the

13 Rydelnik, Michael, and Michael Vanlaningham. 2014. *The Moody Bible Commentary*. Moody Publishers. p. 1463.

sins we commit over and over again, we choose daily to forgive those who have hurt us in the firing process.

Through this process, we might even see that some of our anger toward others does not require our forgiveness, for they have not wronged us. For example, how could I justify being mad at those who continued serving or stayed at the church? It was the advice I gave, the prayers I prayed, and now, I was angry with them for it?

Yet through it all, God showed me who I truly needed to forgive. And as you will read in the last two chapters, the daily choice to forgive brought freedom into my life and positioned me to pursue authentic reconciliation.

Handling Triggers

The concept of a trigger has become a well-understood term in our culture. As a student pastor, I have talked with many students about triggers related to overcoming lust, jealousy, anger, depression, and anxiety. Know your trigger(s). If you find yourself in a situation where a trigger is present, put into place your action steps so your trigger doesn't lead you down the road of regression and regret. Don't allow a thought to dictate feelings and emotions, but actually think about that thought, feel the feelings the thought brings up, and then move forward in living freely, not controlled by any negative thought or emotion. Little did I know there would be very good things in my life that, for a time, would become triggers that brought me back down the path of anger and bitterness.

My first trigger was certain worship songs—the songs we sang at my old church, which my new church also sang. This was hard because most churches that have a contemporary worship style sing many of the same songs. Months into my time at my new church, I stood in our auditorium and entertained negative thoughts about my previous experience—and I mean thinking these thoughts throughout the entire worship set! I couldn't focus on God because these songs were triggers; good, edifying, God-glorifying songs set off my feelings of resentment, anger, and bitterness.

The second trigger was specific "church" words or "church philosophies" that came up in staff meetings. In many Protestant evangelical churches, you hear similar words to describe the church's mission, vision, and values. After being at my new church for almost a year, our church leaders hired a consulting group to help us establish a new vision and mission. Even the word *consulting*, which can be a positive thing, had a triggering effect on my mind. These talks brought me back to my negative experience of "clarifying our mission, vision, and values" with the first consulting group at my previous church.

Unfortunately, singing worship songs and being a part of this new consultation process were not elective activities. I needed to sing worship songs every week; this consulting process was the start of a five-year journey for our church, which I needed to be a part of. So I had two options to deal with these triggers.

Option One: I could leave during the singing portion of the worship service and never engage in musical worship. As well, I could remove myself from any consulting talk and plug my ears during any staff meeting that dealt with our new vision and mission.

Option Two: I could choose to deal with these triggers head-on with God's Word as my weapon of choice for the battle I would daily face.

Trust me, option one was very tempting and something I found myself doing once in a while—not the plugging my ears thing, but the not being in the service during worship. But for God to help me through these triggers, I applied Paul's words when these triggers arose in my mind:

> *"Finally, brothers, whatever is true, whatever is honorable, whatever is just, whatever is pure, whatever is lovely, whatever is commendable, if there is any excellence, if there is anything worthy of praise, think about these things"* (Philippians 4:8).

In those triggering moments, I made the conscious choice (over and over again) to think of the good, the pure, and the lovely. I worshipped God and thought only of Him when we sang similar worship songs at church. Whenever staff or consulting meetings happened, I spent a great amount of time before them praying that God would give me His heart for the current process, not my broken heart from the previous process. God wanted good change to happen in my new church, and I had to see this, believe this, and not allow past wounds to be triggered through this process.

Like many of the things discussed in this chapter, I still struggle with this. Maybe not as much as I did in the first year, but my mind can still be triggered during worship or anytime we talk about mission, vision, and values. However, because I have identified these triggers, I can also, as Paul writes, "Take every thought captive to obey Christ" (2 Corinthians 10:5b). I am more aware of my triggers, and I am able to see them coming and prepare to battle them; I can fight the battle well and avoid going down those dark roads of regret and bitterness by applying God's Word to my thinking.

So when you deal with triggers that lead you back down the path toward anger and bitterness, take the steps to identify them, prepare to battle against them with prayer, and fight those triggers off with God's Word. The hard thing about triggers is they can hide themselves in really good things, things that will be a part of your life for a long time. You probably don't have the option to run away from the good things in your life that are triggering, but God can redeem that negative experience and turn it into something good. He wants to help you through the "trigger" process.

Killing Pride

Wait, what? You're writing about this again?

You bet I am, and here's why: Fifteen months after being fired, there were *five* different people from my former church who reached out to me within the same month. All of them wanted to "catch up" and ask how I was doing. I was doing well with *not knowing* what was going on at my previous church. I had only one or two people I connected with every so often, and we rarely talked about my previous church. I still refrained from engaging with social media and even blocked the old church's website from my computer so that I wouldn't be tempted to see what they were doing or promoting online. But I found it strange that all five people reached out to me in the same timeframe.

One meeting after another, the "catch up" was to inform me that the new youth pastor was taking the student ministry away from the attractional model of ministry and into a more "small group, leader-emphasized" ministry. As these people—two of my former leaders, two pastors at the church, and one of my former students—so eloquently put it, "They are doing what you wanted to do because everything flopped last year in the student ministry." What I heard in those meetings was, "You were right, Kyle. Your supervisor was wrong!" Oh, the sweet-sounding music to my big, prideful ears! One of the pastors even told me how the meeting went when the youth pastor brought this idea up to my former supervisor, asking to change things. There was such overwhelming support from other key leaders and the consultant group for this new ministry shift that my supervisor couldn't say no. In every meeting, I thought of Bart Simpson's "HA-HA!" moments in *The Simpsons* TV show, when he was right and made sure everyone knew about it. I wanted to jump on my old supervisor's desk and go "Bart Simpson" on him.

To be fair, I knew the heart of those people I met with; they wanted to encourage me. Their goal was to let me know that what I was doing was good and that I shouldn't give up on what God has called me to do in my new church and new student ministry. Their aim was honorable. I need to focus on relationships over programs, developing leaders and empowering students instead of being the Billy Graham of the student ministry. But my heart still had little pieces of pride that had not been completely destroyed, and now they were itching to get out.

So I was back at it again—dealing with the painful reality of my pride. I had to get rid of the "I was right; you were wrong" mentality and instead, praise God that things were moving in a healthy direction for everyone involved. When we turn our hearts to praise God, we join Him in stomping out any pride still left in our hearts. I thanked God and prayed for the student ministry at my old church almost daily. I had to choose to celebrate what God was doing instead of being prideful, bitter, or even jealous that the new guy was getting the green light to change the student ministry. Instead of being happy that things did not go well in the previous year because my supervisor's method "failed," I had to choose to thank God that He was and is still doing an amazing work in those students and parents, no matter what ministry philosophy is being practiced.

This battle was hard because my battle with pride has been a long, drawn-out war extending over many years. Even today, as I write, it is hard not to feel the tiny Bart Simpson emotion popping into my heart. But I am reminded of Jesus's attitude, which Paul writes about: "Do nothing from selfish ambition or conceit, but in humility count others more significant than yourselves" (Philippians 2:3). Jesus had every right to hold His "God-ness" over everyone while He was on this earth, but He didn't. So why would I ever have any right to hold something over others, something so minuscule compared to the divinity of Christ? I am no greater than my old supervisor or the new youth pastor, so it doesn't matter what I wanted to do or accomplish at my previous church. That was history, as they say. What matters is that my focus remains on what is best for the students I now disciple, to fall more in love with Jesus and become disciples themselves. God can use *whomever* to help accomplish His plans and purposes. I should be thankful that He even gave me an opportunity to do what I do on this earth.

Toward the end of that first year doing student ministry in a new way, I met with the counseling pastor from my old church for coffee to catch up (we hadn't started our consistent counseling meetings yet). He informed me that recently the senior pastor had shared in one of His sermons that they want to be a church not so prideful as to say there is only one way to do ministry at their church. They need to be a church that is open to new ideas and new ways to engage people. Here's the kicker: the senior pastor even referenced the high school ministry as one way their church was doing that! I couldn't believe it, so I just *had to* watch his entire sermon later. Sure enough, that's exactly what he said!

I went home that day after listening to the sermon and shared everything with my wife. To be honest, my heart was critical, skeptical, and questioning if he, my former supervisor, and the church leaders were really behind this idea. But then the Holy Spirit used my wife as she said this to me: "When you are skeptical of any good change happening, you're not thinking that the person isn't big enough to change. Instead, you're making God out to be too small to change that person." *Ouch.* But she was right, and my pride was (again) in the way of seeing God do this transformation in the hearts of the leaders at my previous church. So I confessed my sin to my wife and to God. Then I praised God for the amazing work He was doing and prayed He would continue to convict me and destroy my pride so I could continue serving and supporting the transformative work He desired to do in everyone.

When you are skeptical of any good change happening, you're not thinking that the person isn't big enough to change. Instead, you're making God out to be too small to change that person.

Watching Instant Replay

In my first interview with a church, the campus pastor who had been fired from his previous church before coming to this new church had told me about this "instant replay" reality. There would be times when he would replay conversations and moments from his previous church and think of new things to say or ways he could've diffused situations or handled things differently. It's a time-killer, an emotion-killer, a spirit-killer, and Satan used these opportunities to leave him feeling defeated, discouraged, and angry by replaying these moments in his mind. I was right there with him, and sometimes, I am still right there with him.

Replaying the past—the "I wish I could've done this or that,"—is not healthy. It can become a trigger, leading you back to pride, bitterness, and anger. It's a detriment to healing spiritually and emotionally. This was especially hard for me in this writing process and even in the journaling process after starting at my new church. Even being six years removed from the beginning of my refined by the fire(d) journey, it can still seem raw to me. Writing and working through all of this is hard. Why? Because I can find myself replaying conversations and proving myself right and my former supervisor wrong instead of doing the redemptive work of writing this book to encourage, heal, and help those who have been fired. And if you're reading this book, journaling, and doing the refined by the fire(d) work, I know it might be hard for you too!

So how do we avoid replaying old conversations? It's like if someone tells you to not think of an elephant, your mind will then only think about an elephant—it's nearly impossible not to!

Many times, these replays begin without a trigger; they just come into our minds. The tactics I shared before for battling triggers can be very helpful. I also dwell on this verse and the concept behind it: ". . . (look) to Jesus, the founder and perfecter of our faith, who for the joy that was set before him endured the cross, despising the shame, and is seated at the right hand of the throne of God" (Hebrews 12:2). Coming on the heels of the "Hall of Faith" chapter, the focus of this verse is about having the faith that ensures true joy can be found in trials and hardships.

As I replay past conversations, I stop myself from debating my former supervisor or proving him wrong, and instead, I thank Jesus for allowing me to go through that conversation and even the firing. I go back to James 1:2–4 and remember those initial lessons God taught me. I praise Him for His faithfulness to remind me of those lessons when the enemy tries to get me to replay conversations. I look at Jesus's example of enduring everything for me, knowing that He would one day be reunited in perfect relationship with the Father and the Spirit in Heaven. I long for that same joy, knowing that how I endure and choose joy and forgiveness over bitterness and resentment is what God desires for me and is what's best for me.

As you have been reading this book and (hopefully) journaling everything the Lord has been teaching you in this process, it can be easy to go back and replay every conversation and think of how you could have proven a point, kept your job, etc. Don't! Instead, thank God for the trial by fire(d) process; praise Him for the work He has done in your heart that might never have taken place if you weren't fired. Take captive any feelings of anger, bitterness, and pride. Refocus those triggers and replays by turning it all over and receiving God's amazing love for you! "Set your minds on things that are above, not on things that are on earth" (Colossians 3:2). The earth, the world, Satan—they want you to live in the past, but God has something greater for you when you focus on the things above, on Him and His presence in your life. Trust the trial by fire(d) process; it really is for your good and for His glory . . . and there is nothing more satisfying than that.

A Note to Leaders

This chapter is just as applicable to the one who was fired as it is to the one who did the firing. You may have your own anger:

> *God, why did I have to manage that employee in the first place?*

You may realize your need to forgive or be forgiven:

> *God, I need to let go of the past hurt and my failures.*

You may have your own triggers:

> *God, why is it hard to* not *think about the past?*

You may struggle with pride too:

> *God, maybe I'm still not leading well for my employees; is that why the same issues keep arising with those I lead?*

You may want to relinquish your own instant replays:

> *God, I know if I would've just said* this *or handled* that *differently, things would be better.*

I would encourage you go back through the process, ask God to reveal anything new, and trust He will refine you and make you a better leader and Christ-follower.

9
PEACE OUT OF THE FIRE(D)

As we moved into the following calendar year, the church I was at was set to enter a new season of ministry. To my surprise—and to many staff and church members' surprise—our senior pastor left our church to move out of state and become a senior pastor elsewhere. Though it was a surprise, I remember that early spring day, when my senior pastor told me he was leaving, realizing God had sovereignly worked to bring me to this church so I could step into the now-open role of senior pastor. I knew at some point in my ministry career, I wanted to be a senior pastor. But I was surprised to have the peace come over me that did at that moment, especially since I didn't think it would happen so soon. I was only thirty-one years old.

My wife and I prayed daily, keeping our thoughts and prayers to ourselves for months until late summer when the position was officially posted. I informed the elders and the search team that I was applying. Throughout those next several months, God gave me favor within my church, with my staff teammates, and with the church leadership. I gained multiple opportunities to preach, along with some other staff, and grew confident in the calling God had placed on my life.

At the end of the year, the search committee announced I was the recommended candidate, and the church would vote on it at the beginning of the new year, the greatest year we've all ever lived—2020! I could list hundreds of stories of how God had prepared me over the years to be a senior pastor and lead a church through a global pandemic, political division, racial injustice, online-only church services, and everything else that year had to offer . . . but that's another story for another time.

It was in this new season I made even more sense of what I had experienced in the past and how I could move forward in ministry without bitterness, frustration, regret, resentment, or plain ignorance about my selfish desires and shortcomings.

Over the course of the past few years as a senior pastor, I've consistently made these four choices when I find my mind or heart back in the fire(d). (I made them back when I was in the heat of my fire(d) season, but I never had this type of clarity or a solid framework of understanding what I should be doing.)

So whether you're on Day 1 of your refining journey (my empathy abounds) or you're still processing the pain of your firing from years ago (you have my compassion), you can start a new path today by making these four choices: seek clarity, pursue harmony, speak honestly, and love unconditionally. No matter why or when the fire glows hot around you, making these choices will help protect you from getting burned, and instead, be refined, growing more Christlike.

And for those who step back into ministry, consider these four actions as part of your daily choices. That way, you don't bring the ashes of your fire(d) season into your new position.

1. Seek Clarity

As hard as it was to sit through those meetings with my former supervisor and feel the betrayal and shame of being fired again, it gave me crystal-clear clarity about what was important and not so important to me. This was helpful for me as I entered the senior pastor search process as a candidate—and even a little when I was hired as the youth pastor a few years before. I knew what I cared about; I knew what energized me, and I knew what I thought was a "win" or "success" in youth and, ultimately, church ministry. With all of this clarity, I clearly articulated my ideas and vision to the search team, then to the staff and the church.

When you get fired and the reasons you hear are generic, vague, or unhelpful—the reasons church leaders are known for giving—don't just sit back and accept them. Lean in and ask the hard questions to seek clarity about why they feel it's necessary to fire you.

When you get fired and the reasons you hear are generic, vague, or unhelpful—the reasons church leaders are known for giving—don't just sit back and accept them. Lean in and ask the hard questions to seek clarity about why they feel it's necessary to fire you.

I recognize my situation was unique; not only did I take my supervisor's notes, but I also went through a mediation process after being fired. I also understand trying to seek clarity in that raw and emotion-filled moment of being fired can be extremely difficult. Your brain and heart are flying in a million directions.

And, of course, for many of you reading this book, your firing experience was some time ago. So let's do some soul-searching together, pulling back the weeds and the overgrowth, and get underneath the surface.

Wait! I thought you said not to go to Instant Replay!

I did. But that was advice related to the purpose of proving your supervisor wrong, not to seek clarity. Give yourself the gift of doing an honest assessment of your time at your previous church. What were the true reasons you were fired? What were the examples given as to *why* you weren't *a good fit*? Are there situations or moments in your time working there that pop into your mind? Write those down—not to beat yourself up but to ask yourself, *What does this reveal about my heart?*

I've written a ton about the pride the Lord revealed to me in my heart, but I also know what I value the most in ministry. What are the things God is revealing to you, now that you might see how you could've handled something differently or responded to someone differently? What are some things He has confirmed in you that you are most passionate about in ministry? Knowing these things before you step into your next role or having a greater awareness of them in your new role or the new season of life will be life-giving to you and those with whom you work. Seek clarity, not only when you're in the fire(d) but also as you take time to reflect on the fire(d).

2. Pursue Harmony

I can't sing, period. I can't carry a tune, play a guitar, or lead the church in singing together. Not only can I not sing well or play an instrument the way it should be played, but I can't harmonize with others. What I mean by that is as everyone is singing different vocal parts to the song (bass, tenor, alto, soprano) to make a beautiful sound, I find myself sounding more like a junior high boy going through puberty. (Oddly enough, the last time I could sing and harmonize was in junior high, but then puberty hit and those dreams were dashed forever.) I can't hear or match the notes other people are singing in any song, which is why I sit in the front row at church, by myself, where I can only hear the worship team singing, and no one can hear me singing.

When you've been fired, it's easy to feel like you are out of tune with everyone else, whether you're still in the firing season or you're bringing some of your unresolved baggage into a new season of life and ministry. Yet it is vital for you to pursue harmony with others, or as Paul writes, "If it is possible, as far as it depends on you, live at peace with everyone" (Romans 12:18, NIV). One of the main things you can do to pursue harmony and peace with everyone is to seek reconciliation with those who have hurt you, including your former supervisor.

I want to take you back to the night before the announcement to my current church that I would become the next senior pastor. I had been feeling a tug from the Holy Spirit for months, a tug that told me I needed to reach out to my former supervisor to let him know I was moving into this role. I felt like I couldn't get in front of people every Sunday, counsel and disciple people throughout the week about the Gospel—this "ministry of reconciliation"—without pursuing reconciliation with him.

So that Saturday night, I finally emailed him, and here's what I wrote:

> *I hope this email finds you well! I know it has been nearly two and a half years since we last spoke to each other. God has worked a ton on my heart and has done some pretty crazy and awesome things in my family's life. He has proven His faithfulness to us over and over again. And I am sure He has done the same for you and your family. I stand in awe of His work and could not imagine being where I am today without God's kindness and faithfulness.*
>
> *This leads me to writing this email, as I feel the Holy Spirit has really impressed this on my heart—to reach out to you. To make a long story, short-ish . . . about 6 months ago, the senior pastor at the church I am at left after being there for 22 years. Maria and I began to seek the Lord about what steps of faith He was asking us to take. Tomorrow, those steps of faith will become a reality, as I will be announced to the church as the next senior pastor. I would not have imagined that I would be stepping into this role, but God's hand has been all over this, and we could not be more excited.*
>
> *So I wanted to reach out and tell you that I am sorry for holding bitterness and anger in my heart toward*

you for quite some time. I know I cannot get up on stage every Sunday and preach a message of forgiveness and reconciliation if, as Romans 12:18 says, "If it is possible, as far as it depends on you, live at peace with everyone." So I want you to know I am sorry for not desiring peace with you, a brother in Christ. I am sorry for any ill will I spoke of you over these past couple of years. I genuinely seek your forgiveness and hope you can forgive me for my sins against you.

I do hope we can grab coffee sometime and pursue some type of reconciliation. I don't know what that looks like, but I know God has impressed [upon] my heart to at least pursue a conversation with you. You don't have to, and that's totally fine. I know with the Christmas season heavy upon us, that probably won't happen until after the New Year.

He responded that Sunday morning with this email:

Great to hear from you! This is meaningful to me that you would reach out. Congratulations on the new opportunity as senior pastor. I'm thrilled for you. Sounds like today is a big day for you. Even as I type this now, I'm praying that the Lord brings favor and increased opportunity for the Gospel through you and your ministry. I would enjoy the opportunity to grab a cup of coffee sometime soon. Please know that I have no ill will against you . . . at all. I believe in you and

> *want the best for you and your family and ministry. I know that [our] re-connecting would honor the Lord.*

A couple of days into 2020, we got that coffee. We spent almost two hours talking, catching up, and honestly, it felt like we were talking and communicating like we had in the first six months that I served under him. I was encouraged, refreshed, and excited to converse with my brother in Christ. In our conversation, I reiterated I was sorry for feeling bitter and angry at him. He forgave me, and he also sought my forgiveness, owning the fact he did not handle things well with me back in those two months and had hurt me during that process. We talked about our families, ministries, being a young leader, and the future vision for the Church (who knew two months later, all of those ideas would be thrown out the window thanks to COVID-19). I left surrendering to the peace of God and truly believing the truth of what my former supervisor wrote in the last line of his email: "reconnecting would honor the Lord."

When I first began writing these stories down, I honestly didn't think I would ever have the courage, let alone the desire, to want to reconcile my relationship with my supervisor. But I realized I was harboring bitterness that was still morphing into anger around those I loved the most. My wife would be the first to share that I have had to work through anger issues ever since I was fired. I was a different person before this firing and am working on releasing that bitterness (daily!), through the power of the Holy Spirit. Though I have made great strides, there is still work to do, but one of those big strides was seeking reconciliation and restoration in my relationship with my former supervisor.

If you are reading this and thinking, "There is no chance I would ever do this . . . they can come to me when they are ready to own up for the hurt they caused me," I would encourage you to evaluate these verses from God's Word that convicted me and showed me I couldn't have this mindset, this heart, moving forward. I had to pursue harmony.

- Romans 12:18: "If possible, so far as it depends on you, live peaceably with all." (Yes, you and I need to read this three times within a few pages. You'll thank me later.)
- Colossians 3:13b: "As the Lord has forgiven you, so you also must forgive."
- James 3:16–18: "For where jealousy and selfish ambition exist, there will be disorder and every vile practice. But the wisdom from above is first pure, then peaceable, gentle, open to reason, full of mercy and good fruits, impartial and sincere. And a harvest of righteousness is sown in peace by those who make peace."

These words, and others, have pierced my soul over the years, reminding me of how important this pursuit should be in my life. There are not only multiple commandments from the Bible to follow up on this (see Matthew 5:25–26 too), but the purpose behind this hard work is for you and I to be released from the chains of bitterness and resentment, which Satan would love to use to keep us in bondage for years to come. He would love to grow anger and bitterness in our lives so that it spews out in the relationships closest to us. That's why it is so important to pursue this type of connection, reconciliation, and restoration.

On my computer desktop, I have this quote from Lewis B. Smedes: "To forgive is to set a prisoner free and discover that the prisoner was you."[14]

I'm not perfect. Even as I write this, I still have my days where I struggle with bouts of anger toward my former supervisor, my old church—just the whole situation. There are days I wish my past looked different from what it does, even though God's faithfulness has been abundantly evident through it all. When these feelings arise, it is important to deal with them head-on, process them, whether with a close friend, mentor, or even a professional counselor. There is a shame that comes upon me when I feel this way: getting angry, jealous, bitter, etc. But I know through the power of the Holy Spirit, I can lean into those feelings and find redemption and freedom on the other side. I'm thankful reconciliation has happened between us, and I have a much better perception of my previous church, but the restoration within and the redemption of my soul are still ongoing. I always teach that forgiveness is a decision, but reconciliation is a process. I firmly believe that is true, but once reconciliation is experienced and achieved, the restorative work that brings freedom is an even longer, harder process, but it's worth it. Pursuing harmony with others is a daily grind, but it is worth it.

---

14 Smedes, Lewis B. 1984. *Forgive and Forget.* p. 53.

If you haven't started the reconciliation process, ask God to give you the courage and grace to reach out and pursue harmony. If the people who hurt you don't respond or reciprocate, all you can do is continue to pray for their hearts to be softened. Through this firing experience, He wants to make you more like Jesus, but don't neglect the work He needs to do in you after this trial. Don't beat yourself up if there are days when it's harder to pursue harmony with others, especially if you have forgiven your employer, but they have not reached back out to you to be reconciled.

This is you pursuing harmony, living at peace with everyone, and doing what you need to do to move forward. Even if the reconciliation can't happen, you can still have the freedom to move forward in the restorative work that God wants to do in your life through forgiveness. Pursue harmony; it will be music to your soul and a sweet sound to those you interact with daily.

3. Speak Honestly

I have shared the importance of speaking honestly from the perspective of church leaders who are making the fire. But it is equally important for the fired individual to speak honestly—about themselves, about their supervisor, and about the church. In the heat of the fire(d), it is important to speak honestly about what is happening while being careful about what is shared or not shared from your experience. Slandering, gossiping, exaggerating . . . there's no place for that in any conversation that you have with others. By God's grace alone, I did this with all the initial conversations I had with students, leaders, parents, and even my supervisor. But as time went on, it was easier to exaggerate (just a tiny bit) or slander the decision-making process and the decision-makers in my former church.

In the winter of 2020, I was having coffee with someone from our church who is also a professional counselor. He was asking about my experience at my former church, and as I briefly shared some details, he stopped me and said, "You're still angry about this, aren't you?"

My immediate response was like the childish response, "No, I'm not angry; you're angry!" Thankfully, I didn't share that out loud; instead, I said, "Well there are days, but we've reconciled . . . we're good."

He responded, "No, you're not good. You may have reconciled, but you're not speaking truthfully about how you feel." Game. Set. Match. I was convicted in the most holy of ways.

And this brought me into a season of digging deeper than just "seeking clarity" about the situation. I talked to my wife about it and in her loving way, she said, "Yes, you're still an angry person, more than you let on to others, and your family feels it the most." Game. Set. Match (again).

I thought I had actually handled the crazy political season well; I thought I was navigating the covid tension of masks or no-masks, "open" the church or "close" the church, social justice, and everything else fairly well, and I was. Don't get me wrong, though, I had my days—like we all do who serve in leadership—but the driving force behind any anger in this season—or the general frustration at home when the kids didn't listen or conflict arose with my spouse—was disproportional to the anger I was expressing, and I was blind to it. I minimized it, blew it off as "not that big of a deal," or I'd say things like, "My tone isn't that loud and angry; you're just overreacting." I had to get honest with myself and where my heart was at . . . and that's when I discovered I still had anger brewing under the surface.

At the beginning of 2021, I reached back out to the counseling pastor (CP) at my former church, who was now semi-retired, and told him where I was at and what this other counselor and Maria had perceived in my heart. So we started meeting twice a month at Panera Bread just talking through how I was feeling and what I was going through at church and at home.

Time and time again, he challenged me to speak honestly, "Go an extra ten percent deeper," to really share what was on my heart or mind and specifically why I was feeling what I was feeling. It was in these times together that I realized I had unresolved anger toward God: anger that He'd brought me through the firing in the first place, anger that my wife was not fully healed yet, anger that my first year as a senior pastor was marred by a worldwide pandemic caused by a scary virus, anger that He would still use my previous church to proclaim the Good News and advance the Kingdom when I wanted to see it burn to the ground (figuratively of course, not literally! Besides stealing, I also don't encourage committing arson).

I didn't (couldn't) get to this place of really working through these feelings and figuring out a better way to handle the anger or frustration in my heart until I spoke honestly about them.

What I learned is that God can handle my honesty, even if I am honestly mad at Him for choosing this part of my story for my life. And when I speak honestly to Him, I can then be honest with others and process my emotions in a healthy way. I don't feel the need to slander or exaggerate because there is nothing to hide. I don't have to paint a better picture of myself or a worse picture of my former church because I know God's heart is good, and His plan is what's best. I'm more aware of my need to lovingly speak my mind at home or with others when I'm initially frustrated, instead of pushing it aside as "not a big deal," and then allowing it to brew in my heart and explode in anger when a different situation doesn't warrant that type of response.

You may have some unresolved issues from your firing, or maybe the firing brought to light something else you need to work through. Whatever it is, speak honestly about how you're feeling. Speak honestly to God; He already knows what your heart is feeling before you even know it. When we choose to speak honestly about what is happening to us in our refined by the fire(d) season, it helps us leave with integrity and uphold the name of Jesus and His Bride. When we speak honestly about how we're feeling after the firing, it allows God to do His refining process and helps us move forward in love, living a life that reflects Jesus to the world, which brings us to the last decision to choose . . .

4. Love Unconditionally

This one is "a lot easier said than done." The last few years are clear examples of how difficult it can be to love others unconditionally in our world.

Left to ourselves, our love is conditional. It is dependent on whether we agree with each other's opinion on anything and everything. And if we don't . . . *Cancelled! Blocked!* I think we would all agree that the Church needs to rise above this cultural expectation to show a better way of living than what we see in the world. That has always been true, but even more so in these past few years. The prevailing opinion is: I'm all for loving others inside and outside the church with no conditions, no strings attached . . . unless they don't agree with everything I believe, say, or do.

As I shared before, my previous church and my current church are about thirty minutes apart. We reach different communities, even though we are all in the western suburbs of Chicago. That was, until *they* decided to plant a campus five minutes away from *my* church. I couldn't believe it the day I saw an ad on Facebook about a new church coming to our area. I was angry—so, so angry—yet I realized this was not how I felt about other churches that plant in our area.

For my entire youth ministry career, I made it a priority to establish relationships with other youth pastors, partnering with them in reaching more students and being a champion for any youth ministry and church in the area. I took the time to invite new youth pastors to our lunches, led the prayer gatherings, and took ownership of combined youth group events. As a senior pastor, I connected to a group of other senior pastors right before the pandemic shut down. Things stalled for a while, but we connected in 2021 once again. And, when I saw the ad, despite my anger, I knew I had to reach out to the campus pastor of this new church campus and invite him to our gatherings.

It was really hard for me to be welcoming, even though there was a previous ministry connection with this new campus pastor. However, I thought about how important it was for me to be connected with others in the area and the love, prayer, and support I felt when surrounded by others in ministry. If I was for *the Church, for the* Kingdom of God, I would love and support any pastor leading a church focused on helping people find and follow Jesus. Was it hard for me to have that initial coffee meeting to connect? Absolutely. Was it hard to not feel regret or jealousy when he was sharing about the great things their church campus was doing to launch? You bet. Those feelings don't necessarily go away (we're human!), but the choice to love unconditionally minimizes those feelings and maximizes God's heart of love working in and through me.

When you choose to love your previous church and its leadership unconditionally, it does not mean you have to be best friends or be their biggest champion. Don't feel bad that you're not taking your former supervisor out to lunch every week or not sharing or liking all of their social media posts. However, when you choose to love unconditionally, you allow God's love for the world to guide your heart and you become thankful for the work He is doing through any leader and in any church. It is easy for our hearts to fall back into bitterness and jealousy, so we have to be *intentional* about choosing to love unconditionally—every day, no matter what.

Don't Delay! Start Today!

These four choices will be life-giving to you in your refining season. I wish I would've had this framework when I first started this journey. Yet, even as I look back over my story, I see how God led me to make these choices. I know for a fact I would not have been equipped to make these choices without consistently humbling myself before God and asking Him for the power and strength to do these hard things. I don't always get it right, but humbling myself in prayer is the fuel that empowers me to make these choices.

Remember my counselor friend, who called me out on my anger? At the end of that meeting, he challenged me to consistently pray for my previous church, that God would bless them and further their mission and reach in *their* community and *my* community. He knew that twice a week, I drive past my previous church on the way to our family's chiropractic appointments.

So now, every time I drive past the church, I take a moment to pray for them. Prayer is what softens our hearts to love; prayer is what draws out bitterness and envy and replaces it with genuine care; prayer is what helps us continue to be refined, even when we don't want to be anymore.

As I finish writing this portion of the book, I am about to head out to one of those appointments and drive past my former church. So I am preparing to pray, which will help me consistently make these four choices today as I find myself faced with the reality of my fire(d). You can do the same! As you pray, journal, and process, I encourage you to not only pray for the power to make these choices but to also write them out, even commit them to memory. You will remember these choices amid your internal dialogue—as well as during any future hard conversations and difficult situations. So what are you waiting for? Start today! Start now!

A Note to Leaders

Just as with the last chapter, if you've fired someone, these four choices can apply to where you are at in your leadership career.

- Do you have clarity about what you're looking for while hiring staff? Have you provided clarity to your current staff regarding what your expectations are for them?

- When you don't get along with your employees, are you making the effort to pursue harmony first, or are you waiting for them to "get on board" or "get on the bus" and follow you without question?
- Do you have your own issues, own *stuff,* that you need to process and work through with a mentor or counselor, perhaps based on how you were previously managed? Are those previous dysfunctions affecting how you are leading today?
- Is your heart filled with conditional, performance-based love for your staff?

Take some time now to think through these questions and choices, and if necessary, seek out trusted counsel and support.

10

LET'S ALL BE REFINED!

When I was in high school, I liked a girl and became good friends with her over a two-year period. I made it clear throughout our friendship that I wanted to be more than friends, but she was content putting me in the infamous "friend zone." Though we connected emotionally, spent a lot of time together, and never hung out one-on-one with anyone else of the opposite gender, we were never officially "boyfriend and girlfriend."

Over time, I lost my interest in her (in *that* way) and liked someone else. Even though we never went "official," I felt the need to tell her I was going to ask this new girl out on a date. In one of the quickest and most awkward conversations of my life, I called her and told her I was going to hang out with this girl and wouldn't be spending alone time with her anymore. There was a long pause. Then she softly said, "OK," and that was it.

After that conversation, I felt weird and confused about it all: the conversation, the friendship, everything. Years later, I realize there was never any closure with my friend. I never got to talk through why we were "breaking up" or not seeing each other anymore. I never got to talk through why she only saw me as a friend but emotionally treated me as her boyfriend. Thankfully, the only physical contact we shared was holding hands on the couch while watching a movie or the good ole Christian-youth-group-approved side hug. Yet I wondered why she wanted that with only a *friend*. I never got answers to these questions, and that's why I say I never had closure for our relationship.

I wish I could finish this book off with "closure." Closure within my own heart, closure by talking with all of my former students and parents, closure in my relationship with God—the list can go on and on. But this scar of being fired will always remain, at least until I see my Savior face to face.

I will never *not* be able to think about this firing. Sure, I assume as time goes on, it will be on my mind less and less. After all, that's been my experience so far. But the lessons I've learned from the Lord in this trial will be lessons I will have to remind myself of throughout the rest of my life.

So I can't give you complete "closure" advice for moving on from your firing, but I hope as I end this book, I can share some final thoughts about the practical side of what supervisors and staff or team members—employers and employees—can do and not do within these work relationships. I have a couple of takeaways for each group and a specific one for other people involved in church (e.g., church members). I know general attendees have a lot to work through, too, when church leadership fires a staff member. I hope this can help you process, grieve, heal, and move forward in life.

Supervisors

One

Work hard *not* to fire someone. About six months into my role in my new church, I was frustrated with the staff person I was supervising. Though he and I had similar personalities and the same ministry mindset, I was struggling to connect with and lead him well as we moved into a new season of student ministry within our church. I left the office one day after a frustrating meeting with him, got into my car, and thought, "It would be so much easier to find someone else for his position."

I couldn't believe it!!! That thought actually crossed my mind! I was less than a year from my firing, and I wanted to move on from my one employee and pick my person. I realized then how easy it is for a supervisor to think this way but how hard it is to work at training and helping our staff become the best they can be at their job (and elsewhere). I vowed in my heart that day that I would work twice as hard on developing my employee as on anything else I did.

How did I do this?

First, I was extremely clear with my expectations. I wanted him to keep track of certain things, like how long each element of youth group lasted, when and where he spent time with students on a weekly basis, what things he was listening to or reading that would help him be a better youth pastor, and more.

Second, I followed up with these items on a consistent basis—at least once a week, sometimes twice a week. No more vague questions, such as "How was your youth group night?" but specific questions where I was looking for specific results.

Third, I prayed for him daily, sometimes in our meeting times but definitely every day in my quiet times.

Through these three actions, I not only witnessed growth in him, but my heart was softened to him. I no longer had thoughts of wanting to replace him, and the Lord killed more pride in my heart.

Supervisors, if you have done those things but you're not seeing the "results" you want, you're *still* nowhere close to firing them. Instead, *you*, not necessarily them, but you must work even harder. The next phase you and your staff member may enter can be called a "probation period" or an "improvement plan." You lay out specific guidelines in writing, which the two of you agree need to be addressed, improved, and/or accomplished to keep the individual with the church. If, after a certain amount of time, they cannot or will not do these things, then maybe it's time to help them transition to what's next for them.

Change takes time, so this cannot be a one- to two-month process. You can't enter this period if you have only been clear about expectations, consistently following up and giving feedback, and praying for them consistently for thirty to sixty days. This should be a long process—one I would recommend is no less than a year. As I said, the hardest work you should do is to avoid firing someone (unless abuse, danger, or a legal/moral issue exists that warrants swift action) because the reward on the other side will be greater.

Think about Jesus and His disciples for a moment. Jesus spent *three years* with them, and they fell short and missed His Kingdom agenda consistently. Even when he stopped speaking in parables and flat-out told them certain things would happen, they abandoned Him. Peter, the person who led Jesus's ministry after His ascension, is the one Jesus spent the most time with, forgave the most, taught and corrected the most, and worked the most and hardest within His three years of ministry. If Jesus did it this way, why should we think we can do it any shorter?

One of my mentors is a senior pastor who hired a youth pastor years ago. After a year and a half, the leadership and senior pastor realized things were not going as well as they wanted with the youth pastor. The leadership and senior pastor spent the next six months working daily with the youth pastor, whether it was with his scheduling, his message preparation, his prioritizing of events, his leadership development, etc. There were clear expectations set for him, and he consistently fell short. So did they fire him? No, not even close.

The next step they took was putting him in this "probation period" I mentioned earlier for an entire year! During this year, they met weekly, talked through expectations on an even deeper level, and got to the heart of why he was doing portions of his job poorly. Over time, both the senior pastor and youth pastor realized the relationship was not working out, that he was not the "right fit for this job," and had lost the passion and desire to be a youth pastor in this season of his life. Once again, instead of just cutting short the year-long probation period, they spent the next six months helping him find a new job outside of church ministry. Toward the end of the year, the church celebrated him and sent him into his new career, with no public communication of his falling short, not being a good fit, not meeting expectations, or any other negative connotations.

Most senior pastors, church leaders, executive pastors, and church employers can sometimes feel like there are more important things to do than train and develop their staff. In fact, most pastoral leaders aren't even trained to lead staff in their undergraduate and seminary education. But as Paul writes to the church in Ephesus, "And he gave the apostles, the prophets, the evangelists, the shepherds and teachers, to equip the saints for the work of ministry" (Ephesians 4:11–12). Those key roles of senior leaders in a church don't necessarily focus on equipping the saints for ministry. Instead of looking at your congregation as the principal people to equip, look at Jesus's model of equipping and focus on your staff.

Jesus spent the most time investing in his disciples, those he "oversaw" for three years. Did He neglect everyone else? Absolutely not, but his primary focus was on those twelve. Let's do the hard work of training and equipping those on our staff because that can be the most rewarding and spiritually fruitful work that you do as a pastor. Lay out clear expectations, walk with your employees who you feel are not meeting expectations, show them what it looks like doing things well, and continue this process with them. Work hard to *not* fire them by working hard to equip them for ministry.

Still not convinced? What if there's a personal benefit to you as a leader? A 2019 *Forbes* article noted multiple studies that revealed the following information:[15]

---

15 Hall, John. "The Cost Of Turnover Can Kill Your Business And Make Things Less Fun." May 9, 2019. www.forbes.com.

- Turnover can cost employers 33 percent of an employee's annual salary. The culprit? The hiring of a replacement. To put a dollar amount on it, if the employee earned a median salary of $45,000 a year, this would cost the company $15,000 per person—on top of the annual $45,000.
- Hiring costs, such as fees to recruiters or advertising, can be pricey. In fact, it's not uncommon for recruiters to request 20–30 percent of a new hire's first-year salary.
- Interview expenses, including travel and the time spent interviewing candidates, pad the costs. So don't neglect to understand post-interview costs, like checking references and administering pre-employment tests. Direct employment costs, such as signing bonuses or relocation expenses, have to be factored in, and that's not even counting onboarding and training.
- There are also some additional hidden costs associated with employee turnover that can harm the workplace. For starters, you're asking your best employees—who are likely already working at full capacity—to either take on the additional tasks the departed employee was responsible for or to show a new hire the ropes.
- It can also do serious damage to morale. If the former employee was close to people who stuck around, those who remain may no longer have that friend at work and become sad or resentful. Others may question whether they should also jump ship.

These are just a few of many reasons why it's more cost-effective and better for your staff, and ultimately for you, to work hard *not* to fire anyone. And because you're a high-level leader, I know that one article or study won't sway your opinion. So, here are a couple more you can look into yourself.[16]

Now, I don't want to give any timeline for how long you should work hard, but I think there is a minimum effort of at least one year to work through this with an employee. The hard work comes in seeking the Holy Spirit's guidance and direction in this process. Even more so, there is a greater effort to send this person off well, to encourage them of their gifts, to celebrate their gifts, and to do everything you can to help them find a new place of work, whether inside or outside of the church.

Be Transformed and Transforming

Supervisors, dream with me for a moment . . . what if churches were known for this type of "firing" process? What if churches did not have to consult outside human resources groups to help weed through the muck of firings, but that outside, business-world, Human Resource departments sought churches to help with these difficult decisions? What if the church looked different from the world in the way we handled firings?

Maybe this is something you have never thought of before, but maybe, just maybe, Jesus's words of being "salt and light" in Matthew 5:13–16 can apply to staff firings. What if this is a clear example of compassion and care that our world needs to

---

16 Reh, John F. "The Cost of High Employee Turnover." August 13, 2019. www.liveabout.com.

Carleton, Cheryl. "Firing Workers Might Cost Them More Than Keeping Them During Coronavirus." April 20, 2020. www.nationalinterest.org.

Lin, Sng Kai. "10 Must-Know Statistics to Inform Your HR Strategy." 2022. www.workstream.us.

see? What if someone who is fired in their business-world job can find rest and solitude and healing and peace by seeing how a church handles a staff firing? The world should see a difference in how the Church does relationships, so put in the hard work before a firing.

But if you do have to fire someone . . .

Two

Be honest, upfront, and compassionate. The unfortunate reality of church firings is that my experience of being slandered and on the receiving end of truth-stretching is common. I am reminded of James's words to teachers in this situation: "Not many of you should become teachers, my brothers, for you know that we who teach will be judged with greater strictness" (James 3:1). The way this verse has always been taught to me is in the context of preaching and teaching false doctrine. But I think there is more to it than false doctrine because as a leader in a church, everything you do or say is a teaching moment. Because you are looked upon as a spiritual leader, any word you speak is a lesson to those around you.

As a parent, you realize this. Your kids are like sponges, and they soak up everything they hear you say. I think of Ralphie from the movie *A Christmas Story*, specifically the scene where his dad hears him say the "*F* word" as they change the flat tire. After being scolded and punished with soap in his mouth, Ralphie tells his mom that he heard that word from his friend. However, everyone knows that he's heard that word, along with many other four-letter words, from his dad—for years! When something doesn't go Ralphie's way, he says that word because his dad had said it hundreds of times, when things weren't going his way.

The people in your church will experience hardships in their life. You will preach sermons or teach lessons that are Bible-based, Spirit-guided, and well-prepared to help people deal with their hardships. But in that moment when you are explaining a firing, they will also be learning how a spiritual leader talks about someone whom they respect and love just as much as you. It will add another formative block to their view of the healthy (or unhealthy) nature of the Church and your church. It will be a positive experience that makes them want to be more like Jesus, or it will turn them away from Jesus and the Church. What you say matters. Choosing to be honest and upfront with your communication about a firing is an exhortation from James to be careful with what you say. You will be held accountable for it.

What you say matters. Choosing to be honest and upfront with your communication about a firing is an exhortation from James to be careful with what you say. You will be held accountable for it.

What does this look like? In my example above about my mentor and his youth pastor, it is being truthful, not slandering, to say someone is pursuing a new position when you have worked with them for eighteen months to help them succeed at their job, helped them find a new job outside of ministry, and championed all of their specific strengths. Without having to share all the details of these difficult situations, supervisors, you can confidently share appropriate truths with your hurting and grieving flock to show them what it looks like to part ways in a healthy way.

Though I think the firing reason of "I'm Paul; your Barnabas, so you're fired" is awful, unloving, and a misuse of that Bible verse, the actual situation as described in Acts 15 gives us a picture of being honest, upfront, and compassionate. After leaving Jerusalem and heading to Antioch to share the decision from the Jerusalem Council, Paul and Barnabas disagree if they should take John Mark with them on their mission to share with the Gentile churches they planted. The text makes it clear that John Mark "withdrawing" (Acts 15:38) from them on their first missionary journey is why Paul doesn't want him with them on their second journey. However, that's all we get. No details. There is no slandering of John Mark's faith, character, competency to be a missionary, or anything else. *And* he is sent out to be a missionary with Barnabas, while Paul and Silas go a different missionary route.

What we don't know from the text is why John Mark "withdrew" from his missionary work on their first journey. What we don't know are the details of the heated exchange or the "sharp disagreement" (Acts 15:39) between Paul and Barnabas. What the Bible doesn't tell us is that Paul was in the right and Barnabas was in the wrong or vice versa. There's none of that; yet, there was honesty in what happened. They were upfront about why this happened, and they had the compassion to help send John Mark out for missionary work and affirm his calling.

Can I ask it again? What if churches and church leaders were known for this type of firing process in our dog-eat-dog business world? What if HR departments looked to churches for how to handle these situations? What if leaders taught their people what honesty and compassion look like in really difficult situations?

As I have said from the beginning, firings will happen in our church context. But we need more Paul and Barnabas stories and less "I'm Paul; your Barnabas, so you're fired" stories. We need more supervisors who will be honest and upfront with everyone when a firing happens. We need more leaders who truly show care and compassion to those being fired by helping them find that next place to work and taking care of any needs they and their families may have in this season. When supervisors do that, then Jesus's words will ring true for us all: "By this all people will know that you are my disciples, if you have love for one another" (John 13:35).

Staff

One

Focus on your heart foremost. This concept developed in my heart when I had that initial conversation with my youth pastor the day after my first firing. God wanted to focus on *me* and the sin in *my* heart that was keeping *me* disconnected from Him. Remember that this trial by fire(d) process is for God to do a refining work in your heart, so lean into that the most. Keep that your highest priority and never keep the refining microscope off your heart.

Two

Let God work on changing other people's hearts. As much as God wants to work on you, He has that same desire to work on your supervisor, the people in your church, and others who are affected by your firing. So let God do His refining work in them and don't try to be God in their lives. I couldn't change my supervisor's heart and attitude in this season; only God could. Though there were many times I prayed for his heart to be softened, I could not change his heart. And though there were many people I consoled and mourned with during this season, I could not change their hearts. But God could, He did, and He will do that work in your situation inside those around you, just as Paul affirmed in his letter to the church in Philippi: "And I am sure of this, that He who began a good work in you will bring it to completion at the day of Jesus Christ" (Philippians 1:6). Let God change hearts while you focus on allowing God to change *your* heart.

Three

Don't lose your dependency on God. It will be very easy to go back into self-sufficiency mode after you find yourself in a new position in ministry or in the business world. As much as you depended on God in the trial, increase that dependency on Him in your new season. Remind yourself of how He was faithful and get on your knees to plead with Him about what He wants to continue to do in your heart and life. When you lack dependency on God, repent and remind yourself that, as Jesus says: "I am the vine; you are the branches . . . apart from me, you can do nothing" (John 15:5).

Global and Local Church-Goers

As a reminder, the capital-*C* Church defines everyone who is a Christian worldwide. The lowercase-*c* church defines your local church gathering, the people within your church building.

The one encouragement I would have for those who are in the church and experience a supervisor firing a ministry worker is to not give up on the Church. The Church has always been and will always be broken. Regardless, never give up on the Church. The people, the church, and the Church are full of sinful, broken people who Jesus loves, died for, and rose again to redeem and restore to perfection. Yet that perfection won't take place until we have passed on from this world. So that means that brokenness will rear its ugly head sometimes, and it seems to especially like to come out during firings. Even so, don't give up on the Church, and don't give up meeting regularly with people in a church.

There is one question that typically comes up in your mind when something like this happens or happens over and over again in your church: should you leave the church or stay with the church? This is a difficult decision because one of the main reasons you have stayed connected at a church is because of the relationships you have with people in the church. The pastors' teaching, the worship music, and some of the ministries for you or your kids may have been what attracted you to the church in the first place, but the people, the relationships, are what have kept you connected. A decision to stay or go will impact your relationships with the people in your church foremost.

I don't have an answer either way for this question, and as I encouraged my high school ministry leaders, do not make a decision immediately after you learn about a firing. Take the time to grieve with those you are close to at the church; process and talk with them, and seek the Holy Spirit's guidance and direction in this decision (yes, pray corporately with them, not just by yourself or with your spouse only). Then, in the subsequent season of searching, look for a couple of things that might help you inform your decision moving forward.

One

Look for humility in leadership. If in your conversations with the leadership, you sense humility or empathy or a desire to understand your viewpoint, see this as a transforming work of the Holy Spirit in your church. Be optimistic about this and pray that God gives them a desire to pursue a healthier process of firing in the future.

Two

Look for a healthy change in the church. If in a few months, the same thing is happening, that's not good. But if there are small steps of change happening, be encouraged and excited! Celebrate the healthy change!

Three

Do the hard work of staying. Just like supervisors need to do the hard work of *not* firing, you can do the hard work of *staying* by showing forgiveness, letting go of bitterness, and believing the best in your leaders.

With all that said, I wouldn't encourage anyone to leave immediately. This is a process that you and your family need to go through. I am thankful for the many people from my previous church who decided to stay because it made them better followers of Jesus. I also know there were some who did leave and found a new church where they could get a fresh start and renew their hope in church leadership. I am thankful for them, too, because they left well and worked through those three steps openly and honestly, seeking the Holy Spirit's leading every step of the way.

Whatever you do, don't lose hope in the beautifully broken Church; don't give up on participating in church consistently, and don't miss the opportunity to pray and work through the decision to stay or find a new church.

Conclusion

ONE HOPE

My hope, born from that first weekend after being fired, was that my story could be of great benefit to the Church: the leaders and employers, the pastors and employees, the volunteers and members, to everyone who is a part of God's Plan A for bringing the message of salvation and redemption to the world. I hope my story has helped you and will continue to help you whenever and wherever you are in the "trial by fired" process.

I also hope my story will make you fall more in love with Jesus, be more thankful to God for your trials, and grow your faith through the refining process God has you in, making you more dependent on the Holy Spirit—for the rest of your life.

Thank you for reading, processing, journaling, and leaning into what God has for you through my story. May it make the Church shine brighter in this dark world, and may God get all the glory for His work in our lives. Amen.

ACKNOWLEDGMENTS

To my wife Maria, thank you for your encouragement, support, and wisdom throughout the book writing and publishing process. We've grown so much closer to each other and to Jesus in our "Wilderness" season and I couldn't imagine my life without you. I love you always n' forever.

To my children, Nora and Max, thank you for being an example of child-like faith every day in our home. Your faith in Jesus inspires me and I pray this season in our family's life would always serve as a reminder of God's faithfulness to you and to us. I love you and am so proud to be your daddy. It's my favorite "job" in the whole world!

To Sophie June, this book would've stayed a personal journal had it not been for you. I love you and cannot wait to meet you someday in eternity. [For more information about Sophie June, visit www.kyleisabelli.com/post/a-book-by-sophie-june]

To my parents, thank you for always praying, always believing, always encouraging, always caring, always reflecting the love of Jesus to me and everyone around you.

I love you and it is an honor to be an Isabelli because of you two.

To Aunt Lisa, Uncle Bruce, Uncle Matt, Grandpa Kevin, and Grandma Lynne, thank you for your love, encouragement, and support to Maria, the kids, and me during this season. It is a tremendous blessing to call you sister, brothers-in-law, and in-laws . . . to call you *family*. Words cannot fully express the impact you continue to have on us throughout every season we've been through.

To J-Laib, thank you for always speaking the truth in love with me in every circumstance in my life. You have been whom I look up to for the last twenty years and I thank God for the example you have shown me to be more like Jesus. Without your advice to be self-reflective and write in a journal, this book wouldn't have been a reality. Your impact for Jesus and His Kingdom is greater than you will ever know on this earth.

To Tom, thank you for processing my pain and grief with me from the beginning. I know I am one of many who have benefitted from your Godly wisdom and counsel and I cherish every time we get to talk, to listen, to cry, to pray and to remain hopeful in God's work in our lives, our family's lives and in the Church.

To the leaders, staff and my entire church family at Avenue, you have no idea how important your acceptance and care was to my family as we came in very broken and very hurt as the Student Pastor in 2017. You have faithfully and lovingly walked alongside us in every season these last several years. I count it one of my greatest privileges and joy to be your Senior Pastor. Thank you for helping me experience the new life, the best life, one that only Jesus could give us—together.

To Caleb Breakey and Eric and Savannah Young, the "Speak It to Book" team and the Author Gateway Writer's Cohort, thank you for helping me see my story was worth sharing, for your compassion and care in the cohort, and for your wisdom, feedback, and guidance to keep refining, keep editing, and keep persevering with my story and proposal so that it can help to redeem the culture around us.

Finally, to the Morgan James Publishing team: Thank you, Isaiah Taylor, for believing in and advocating for my manuscript. Thank you, Cortney Donelson, for helping me write as a writer, not as a speaker. Thank you, Gayle West, for being a joyful and helpful part of every step in this book publishing process. Thank you, David Hancock and Jim Howard, for your wisdom and leadership to me and all the MJP authors. I would recommend working with MJP to any new author who has a story to tell.

ABOUT THE AUTHOR

Kyle Isabelli knows firsthand the pain, grief, and shame that comes with being fired from a church ministry position. He's not only experienced it personally, but he's witnessed fellow staff members and beloved pastors go through similar situations. Through it all, Kyle learned to process his pain and came through his firing with a passion to help hurting staff and care for disillusioned congregants. He has shared his wisdom on podcasts and has counseled dozens of church leaders navigating forced staff transitions. Kyle has been in full-time ministry for over ten years and currently serves as the senior pastor of a church in the western suburbs of Chicago, where he resides with his wife, Maria, and their two children.

Printed in the USA
CPSIA information can be obtained
at www.ICGtesting.com
JSHW020739221223
54184JS00002B/21

9 781636 981864